WORDS AND WOMEN

WORDS and WOMEN

Updated

Casey Miller
and Kate Swift

HarperCollins*Publishers*

WORDS AND WOMEN was originally published by Anchor Press/Doubleday.

"The Awful German Language" is from *A Tramp Abroad* by Mark Twain.

Chapter 5 in slightly altered form first appeared in *The Christian Century.* Copyright © 1976 by Christian Century Foundation, reprinted by permission.

Designed by Cassandra J. Pappas

ISBN: 0-06-096593-2

Library of Congress 90-56094

92 93 94 95 CC/AG 10 9 8 7 6 5 4 3 2

To L.G.M. and E.L.S.

Let the meaning choose the word, and not the other way about.

—George Orwell,
"Politics and the English Language"

CONTENTS

FOREWORD

We need language as much as we need air in order to survive. Air makes physical life possible, language cultural life. Stupidly, we tend to abuse and take them both for granted. We buzz on as if they were the perfect servants—useful, neat, cheap, tireless, loyal, and invisible.

Fortunately, we correct some bad habits. Just as we listen to ecologists who tell us to stop polluting air, we attend to writers who push language into literature, linguists who analyze the complexity of syntax, grammarians who rebuke slovenly and slipshod practices. Since the 1960s, we have also benefited from an extraordinary international language reform movement built on two great principles: 1) The roles of men and women, the gender structures that define "femininity" and "masculinity," are changing. This process is good if and when it augments the well-being and just authority of women; 2) Language, the sign system that defines our realities, reflects and guides this change. Indeed, some believe that symbols and discourse regulate our outer and inner life. If so, a language reform movement is less reform than revolution.

Linguists, philosophers, psychologists, literary critics, public speakers, and writers have participated in this movement. Their lineage includes anyone who has rebelled against linguistic customs that demean women. Why, these rebels have asked, should the God of common prayerbooks have only "Sons" and not "Children" of both sexes? Such rebels have also queried cultural customs that distrust and silence women as public voices. Why, they have asked, should women not preach as well as pray?

Given the scope of the movement, reformers inevitably quarrel about language and its relationships to gender and sexual difference. One especially vexed question is whether the structure of language is such that it is literally incapable of expressing the female and her experience. Must language repress the female in order to operate? If women were to speak without masquerading as men, would they use a separate language *because* they were women? Does sexual difference necessarily entail linguistic difference? A mother's tongue that is separate from a father's linguistic laws? In the 1970s, a number of brilliant French writers began to experiment with "écriture féminine," a writing meant to reveal and express a newly freed woman's body and sensibility. Moreover, if women were to speak as feminists, members of a political and social movement, would they provide a new lexicography? Reasoning that they would, in 1985 Cheris Kramarae and Paula A. Treichler published *A Feminist Dictionary,* which lists many reform resources. In 1987, Mary Daly, "in cahoots" with Jane Caputi, brought out the ebullient *Websters' First New Intergalactic Wickedary,* a "Metapatriarchal Dictionary."

Words and Women: New Language in New Times, which first appeared in 1976, is a central text. So, too, is an article, "One Small Step for Genkind," which Casey Miller and Kate Swift had published four years earlier. Witty but principled, tart but humane, lucid but learned, Miller and Swift addressed a large public about a fundamental question: How can women and men speak to each other, about each other, with dignity, accuracy, and respect?

This public, this question, and the pragmatic wisdom of *Words and Women* are still alive. Some of our most powerful writers mourn the general inadequacy of language. In "Burnt Norton," T. S. Eliot vows that words "slip, slide, perish/ Decay with imprecision." Miller and Swift document another, more specific difficulty: the sexism of our speech. For example, we permit "semantic polarization," in which we use masculine words to convey good meanings, feminine words to convey bad and obscene meanings. Similarly, our speech can be racist. We make "white" words articulate the good, "black" the bad and dangerous.

We also use "the generic he," in which man, but one of two sexes, becomes all of humanity, a masculine noun or pronoun a reference to the entire universe. I grew up with such textbooks as *Man and His World* or *Man and His Values,* which were meant to describe everyone's history and beliefs. Because it presumes that men are the norm, the "generic he" rightly irritates a number of feminists of both sexes. In the early 1970s, while Miller and Swift were working on *Words and Women,* the poet Muriel Rukeyser was composing her poem "Myth," a tough-minded rewriting of the legend of Oedipus. Here Oedipus, "old and blinded," revisits the Sphinx. "When you say Man," Oedipus tells the Sphinx, "you include women/too. Everyone knows that." The Sphinx answers sardonically, "That's what/you think."

Miller and Swift, however, optimistically remind us of our cultural powers. They believe that we language-users have an interactive relationship with our tough but malleable symbols. They shape us; we shape them. In part because of this relationship, the history of language combines continuity with change. Language in the British Isles altered dramatically as it absorbed Celtic, Latin, Anglo-Saxon, and Norman French. The result, English, grew and altered as it became a global language, a part of North America, Africa, India, Southeast Asia, Australia, and New Zealand. Without ripping up syntax, without abolishing noun and verb, we can now change language by purging it of a demeaning, destructive sexism. We can find new words for a more equitable society in which both women and men will speak freely, in which both women and men will make linguistic rules. Indeed, Miller and Swift show people finding such words and building such a society—in publishing houses, churches, novels, and everyday life. A Postscript offers their own proposals for a revivified speech.

In the reformers' quarrels about language and gender, Miller and Swift are sensible moderates. For them, the deep structure of language is gender-neutral. Of course, a masculinist society has different habits of language for men and women. However, we can move language and ourselves beyond all this. So doing, we will realize that women and men are more similar than dissimilar. More unites than separates them. Our language can express this happy commonality.

Despite their common sense and moderation, despite the freshness of the intellectual air they breathe, Miller and Swift have provoked a few hot responses. Some people have accused them of desecrating language, as if language were a changeless, sacred temple, not the grubby, beautiful cultural terrain in which we dwell. Others have charged them with doing away with womanliness and manliness, as if "womanliness" and "manliness" were also changeless, sacred temples, not patterns of behavior that various societies construct and reconstruct. Still others have labeled Miller and Swift humorless. *Words and Women* itself is the most convincing answer to these silly outcries and anxieties. It asks us to think about language and the future cleanly, intelligently, confidently. New words, new women—as Miller and Swift show, these are among the gifts of the twentieth century to the future.

CATHARINE R. STIMPSON
Rutgers University

Preface

Thinking about language is a little like looking into the Grand Canyon: it is as though another vast chasm has opened, this time to the core of civilization where one sees millenniums of human history instead of eons of geologic time. There, embedded in the world's languages, is a record of war and conquest, exploration and assimilation, tragedy and triumph. And there, too, is a record of the distortion and denial of women's experience and the part women have always played in the human enterprise.

Only in the last decades of the twentieth century, as we approach the start of another millennium, are significant numbers of people beginning to examine and challenge linguistic artifices that oppress women. On the frontiers of this long-overdue endeavor are poets and theorists who have chosen to dismantle both syntax and lexicon as they defy established meanings, often using audacious puns and punctuation to suggest alternative insights into the human condition. They are among the many critical thinkers who in probing the psychosexual origins of patriarchal systems have begun to examine patterns of thought and behavior, codified in language, that threaten the well-being, perhaps even the existence, of life on earth. Still others, working at a more pragmatic level, have chosen to concentrate on the ordinary discourse people use daily in all forms of written and spoken communication.

In writing *Words and Women,* first published in 1976, we chose the latter approach. That was because we looked at language not from the point of view of theorists or scholars, but as editors whose craft depends on a healthy skepticism about what this word or that will actually convey to others as distinguished from what we have been taught it should convey. Moreover, as editors called on to deal with a variety of subjects, we were committed to reaching the widest possible audience, including people of both sexes in a range of ages. The result is a plea for language reform, not revolution—although we believe that radical change in the symbolic system of words is inevitable.

The book's original Preface, which follows, describes the circumstances twenty years ago in which we first thought about the sexist nature of standard English. A year and a half later we put those thoughts into an essay published in the *New York Times Magazine* under the title "One Small Step for Genkind," and that effort, in turn, led to the writing of *Words and Women.* Because both article and book took shape at a time when the negative messages standard English conveys to and about women were still largely unacknowledged, we have made the essay a part of this volume. For similar contextual reasons, we have made no substantive revisions in the book, but instead have amplified the Notes whenever circumstances required further comment.

C.M. AND K.S.
1990

Preface to the Original Edition

This book began, in our heads though not on paper, in the fall of 1970. As freelance editors we had been asked to copy-edit a junior high school sex education course designed for church-related youth groups. Knowing the publisher, we felt reasonably certain we would be sympathetic to the author's general approach, and as we guessed, the point of view was objective; the material was straightforward but not unnecessarily clinical; the emphasis was on respect for other people as fellow human beings; and the arguments in favor of sex education in a religious context were convincing. In the author's words, "The objective of the course is simple: to provide a framework in which a teacher and a group of students may explore together what it means to be male and female persons."

We had not been working on the manuscript long, however, when we discovered that whatever the author's intentions, the message coming through was that girls are not as important, responsible, or self-sufficient as boys or as healthy in their outlook on life. This impression was conveyed in part by the materials, both secular and religious, around which the course was structured, but it was also communicated by the standard English the author used.

Beyond raising questions for the author and house editor to deal with as they saw fit, we could not do much about the course materials, but we could and did recast the unconsciously sexist language. As is usually the case in freelancing, many of our suggestions were accepted and many were not, but in the meantime something had happened to us; for as we worked on a critique of the manuscript to justify the editorial changes we were suggesting, we found ourselves thinking about the sexist nature of accepted English usage.

If, as in this sex education course, the objective was to give both girls and boys a healthy sense of their own worth without belittling the worth of the other sex, then standard English set many traps: the shortcut masculine generic words were loaded; the habit of always saying "male and female," "husbands and wives," "men and women" revealed an unquestioned priority; and the words most commonly used to describe females and males were (and are) so burdened by cultural stereotypes as to make them worse than useless in trying to get at what it means to *be* a female or a male person.

Insights like these, once glimpsed, do not go away. We had been sensitized, and from then on everything we read, heard on the radio and television, or worked on professionally confirmed our new awareness that the way English is used to make the simplest points can either acknowledge women's full humanity or relegate the female half of the species to secondary status. Since we ourselves had for years been innocently using the words and grammatical forms that devalued members of our own sex, it was obvious that the process at work was both subtle and powerful and that men were not its only perpetrators.

We also began to discover that we were far behind many

others in our newly acquired awareness of linguistic sexism. Women of as widely diverse interests as the author Dorothy L. Sayers, the historian Mary Beard, and the musicologist Sophie Drinker had discussed the problem in books published in the 1930s and 1940s. Ruth Herschberger provided a brilliant semantic analysis of the patriarchal teaching of human physiology in her book *Adam's Rib,* published in 1948.

Men, too, had been sensitive to the issue. Lynn White, when president of Mills College in the 1950s, wrote of the use of masculine generic pronouns, "The penetration of this habit of language into the minds of little girls as they grow up to be women is more profound than most people, including most women, have recognized; for it implies that personality is really a male attribute, and that women are a human subspecies. It would be a miracle if a girl-baby, learning to use the symbols of our tongue, could escape some unverbalized wound to her self-respect; whereas a boy-baby's ego is bolstered by the pattern of our language."[1]

Others had gone on to question whether little girls would always have to grow up with such a distorted tongue. Eve Merriam included a chapter called "Sex and Semantics" in *After Nora Slammed the Door,* published in 1964. "The discarding of outworn language symbols may force us to think in new ways and so discover solutions to the inequities that persist in our post-emancipated age," she said, with more prescience than most people were then able to recognize.

By the late sixties those looking for solutions to sex-based inequities had begun to discard outworn linguistic symbols in their own writing and speaking and were explaining why. As Wilma Scott Heide of the National Organization for Women put it, "In any social movement, when changes are effected, the language sooner or later reflects the change. Our approach is different. Instead of passively noting the change, we are changing language patterns to actively effect the changes." One of the activists, Mary Orovan, published a pamphlet called "Humanizing English" in which she proposed alternatives to the generic masculine nouns and pronouns. Another activist, Varda One, suggested antidotes to the sex bias of English in a column called "Manglish," which appeared regularly in the periodical *Everywoman.* Articles on linguistic sexism by Jennie Bull, Julie Coryell, Dana Densmore, Jean Faust, Emily Toth, and many others appeared in feminist publications, and Ann Sheldon launched a series of letters to editors satirizing sexist usage.

At about the same time, educators like Alleen Pace Nilsen and others concerned with sexism in children's books and textbooks were beginning to focus on the language problem. Elsewhere in the academic world, Mary Ritchie Key, Haig Bosmajian, and Robin Lakoff were raising the issue in departments of linguistics and speech. Ethel Strainchamps, author of the chapter on language in the milestone anthology *Women in Sexist Society* (1971), had for years been looking at English dictionaries and studies of the language with a critical and feminist eye; and as a working lexicographer, Alma Graham was building the head of steam that powered her contributions in the seventies to the American Heritage dictionaries and the McGraw-Hill Book Company's "Guidelines for Equal Treatment of the Sexes."

The first such guidelines to gain national recognition were published in California in 1972. Designed for authors and editors of social studies textbooks, they were written by Elizabeth Burr, Susan Dunn, and Norma Farquhar, who made the point in their introduction that "a language is not merely a means of communication; it is also an expression of shared assumptions. Language transmits implicit values and behavioral models to all those people who use it."

It was also in 1972 that Haig Bosmajian, writing in *ETC.*, a journal of general semantics, discussed the effect of language on women's sense of identity. "[T]he 'liberation' of women," he said, "the eradication of the sexual subject-master relationship, will have to be accompanied with a conscious effort on the part of women to allow themselves to be defined by men no longer."

Among these pioneers, professional language scholars were in the minority. Most of those thinking and writing about linguistic sexism before the 1970s approached the subject from their own perspective as historians or students or observers of the current scene, and they drew on the springs of their own experience. That has also been our approach. We have culled our examples from a miscellaneous assortment of the books, newspapers, magazines, and television programs we see in the natural course of events. If this approach is unscholarly, it also has advantages, for the random nature of our sources demonstrates the pervasiveness of the problem.

Linguists are said to be amused at partisan efforts to influence language just as doctors are amused at the joke about the man who, since he had no money for an operation, offered his physician a small fee to touch up the X-ray. The analogy, from our point of view, is not persuasive. Sexist words and usage reveal sexist assumptions much as an X-ray reveals a tumor, but there the similarity stops: to paint out the tumor on the X-ray film cannot affect the body, but to consciously discard semantic symbols of deeply rooted cultural assumptions will, we think, help in time to free us from their power.

It may be asked why we chose throughout this book to refer to women as "they" rather than "we." Our answer is one Elizabeth Janeway made at a conference on women in the arts some years ago. Using "they" helps maintain distance, she said. Since we are women writing on a subject that in the short run divides the sexes—though in the long run it should unite them—and since we do not claim to be nonpartisan and were not always cool, we needed the objectivity "they" encourages. More important, as Elizabeth Janeway also said, there is a bigger "we" than women. One of the assumptions we have made is that in our shared humanity the two sexes are more alike than they are different. So although we write out of our experiences as women, we think as human beings and have used "we" in the following chapters only when it stands for all of us.

Still speaking as authors, we are glad to have this chance to thank the many friends, both from the past and the present, who have influenced our thinking and helped us achieve perspective. We are grateful to everyone who sent us material or read and criticized the manuscript. We cannot name them all, but we are especially indebted to Virginia Barber, Jennifer Chatfield, Betsy Cobb, Alma Graham, Ruth and James Oliver, Catherine Pessino, Paula and Alan Schwartz, Sheila Tobias, Carl Viggiani, and Nancy Wilson. It is they who encouraged us to write the book in the first place or who stood by us during the frequent moments when we were not sure it would ever be completed. Many of the mistakes they and our other friends tried to keep us from making we made anyway, but they saved us from making many more.

CASEY MILLER AND KATE SWIFT
1975

Chapter 1

Beginning with Names

The photograph of the three bright, good-looking young people in the Army recruitment ad catches the eye. All three have a certain flair, and one knows just by looking at the picture that they are enjoying life and glad they joined up. They are typical Americans, symbols of the kind of people the modern Army is looking for. The one closest to the camera is a white male. His name, as can be seen from the neat identification tag pinned to the right pocket of his regulation blouse, is Spurgeon. Behind him and slightly to the left is a young black man. He is wearing a decoration of some kind, and his name is Sort—. Perhaps it is Sorter or Sortman—only the first four letters show. A young woman, who is also white, stands behind Spurgeon on the other side. She is smiling and her eyes shine; she looks capable. She is probably wearing a name tag too, but because Spurgeon is standing between her and the camera, her name is hidden. She is completely anonymous.

The picture is not a candid shot; it was carefully posed. The three models were chosen from thousands of possible recruits. They are the same height; they all have dark hair and are smiling into the camera. They look like students, and the copy says the Army will pay 75 percent of their tuition if they work for a college degree. It is no accident that two are white, one black, or that two are male, one female. Nor is it an accident that Spurgeon stands in front of the others at the apex of a triangle, or that, since someone had to be anonymous, the woman was chosen.[1]

In our society women's names are less important than men's. The reasons why are not hard to identify, but the consequences for both men and women are more far-reaching than members of either sex, with a few notable exceptions, have been prepared to admit or even, until recently, to examine. Like other words, names are symbols; unlike other words, what they symbolize is unique. A thousand John Does and Jane Roes may live and die, but no bearer of those names has the same inheritance, the same history, or the same fears and expectations as any other. It therefore seems legitimate to ask what effect our naming customs have on girls and boys and on the women and men they grow into. Are the symbol-words that become our names more powerful than other words?

Few people can remember learning to talk. The mystery of language is rarely revealed in a single moment of electrifying insight like Helen Keller's, when suddenly, at the age of seven, the deaf and blind child realized for the first time the connection between the finger signals for w-a-t-e-r her teacher was tapping into her palm and "the wonderful cool something" that flowed from the pump spout onto her other hand.[2]

From what scholars report about the way children normally acquire speech, it seems probable that "learning to talk" is actually the measured release, in conjunction with experience, of an innate capacity for language that is common to all human beings.[3] We are no more likely to remember the process than we are to remember growing taller. What one may remember is a particular moment—seeing the yardstick exactly even with the latest pencil line marking one's height on the door jamb or learning a word for some particular something one had been aware of but could not name: tapioca, perhaps, or charisma, or a cotter pin. Anyone who has ever said, "So *that's* what those things are called," knows the experience.

When children are first learning to talk they go through a series of similar experiences. The very act of learning what a person or thing is called brings the object into the child's ken in a new way. It has been made specific. Later, the specific will also become general, as when the child calls any small, furry animal a "kitty." Words are symbols; their meanings can be extended.

Amanda, who is twenty months old, has spurts of learning names. "Mum," she says to her mother while pointing to the box. "Mum," she says again, pointing to the doorknob. "What is it?" she is asking without using words. "Tell me its name." When she calls her mother by a name, she knows her mother will respond to it. She knows that she, Amanda, has a name. It is important to her, for she has already become aware of herself as a thing different from everything else. As a psychologist might put it, her ego is emerging. Hearing her name, being called by it, is part of the process.

Amanda makes certain sounds, naming food or her bottle, that tell her parents she is hungry or thirsty. Before long she will speak of herself in the third person: "'Manda want apple." "'Manda come too." She may repeat her name over and over, perhaps mixing it with nonsense syllables. It is like a charm. It may be the first word she learns to spell. She will delight in seeing the letters of her name, this extension of herself, on her toothbrush or drinking mug. They belong to her, not to her brother or to her mother or father.

When children begin to play with other children and when they finally go to school, their names take on a public dimension. The child with a "funny" name is usually in for trouble, but most kids are proud of their names and want to write them on their books and pads and homework. There was a time when older children carved their names or initials on trees. Now that there are so many people and so few trees, the spray can has taken over from the jackknife, but the impulse to put one's identifying mark where all the world can see it is as strong as ever. The popularity of commercially produced name-on objects of every kind, from tee-shirts to miniature license plates, also attests to the importance youngsters (and a lot of grown-ups too) place on claiming and proclaiming their names.

Given names are much older than surnames, of course, probably as old as language itself. One can imagine that as soon as our ancient forebears started using sounds to represent actions or objects, they also began to distinguish each other in the same way. One might even speculate that the people who most often assigned sounds to others were those who produced and cared for the group's new members. Commenting on the assumption of philologists that the exchange of meaningful vocal sounds began among males as they worked and hunted together—hence the so-called "yo-heave-ho" and "bow-wow" theories of language origin—Ethel Strainchamps, a psycholinguist, notes that most philologists have in the past been men. Considering the importance to human survival of communication between mother and child when open fires, venomous reptiles, and other hazards were everywhere, "it might have occurred to a woman that a 'no-no' theory was more likely," Strainchamps says.[4] Perhaps her suggestion should be taken a step further: who knows that it was not the creative effort of women, striving to communicate with each new baby, calling it by a separate and distinguishing sound, that freed the primordial human mind from the prison of animal grunts and led in time to the development of language?

Inevitably, some people dislike the names they have been given, and many children go through a phase of wanting to be called something else. For no apparent reason Anne announces that her name is really Koko and she will not answer to any other. For months nothing will change her resolve. She is Koko—and then one day she is Anne again. But if Cecil decides he wants to be called Jim, or Fanny elects to be known as Jill, the reasons may be less obscure: names do seem to give off vibrations of a sort, and other people's response to your name becomes a part of their response to you. Some psychologists think that given names are signals of parental expectations; children get the message and act on it either positively or negatively. One study claims to show, for example, that names can be "active" or "passive." If you call your son Mac or Bart he will become a more active person than if you call him Winthrop or Egbert. Your daughter is more likely to be outgoing and confident, according to this theory, if you call her Jody rather than Letitia. It follows, though, that if Jody prefers to be called Letitia, she is letting it be known that she sees herself in a more passive and dependent way than you anticipated.[5]

Last names, too, can be positive or negative. Some carry a mystique of greatness or honor: Randolph, Diaz, Morgenthau, Saltonstall. Others are cumbersome, or they invite cruel or tasteless jokes. Many people decide, for one reason or another, to change their last names, but a great many more take pride today in being identified as a Klein or a Mackenzie, a Giordano or a Westervelt. The first-and-last-name mix that a person grows up with—that combination of particular and general, of personal and traditional—is not lightly exchanged for another.

Whether a name is self-chosen or bestowed at birth, making it one's own is an act of self-definition. When a former Cabinet member who had been involved in the Watergate scandal asked the Senate investigating committee to give back his good name, he was speaking metaphorically, for no one had taken his name away. What he had lost, justly or unjustly, was his public image as a person of integrity and a servant of the people. One's name also represents one's sense of power and self-direction. "I'm so tired I don't know my own name" is a statement of confusion and fatigue. *Your* name, the beginning of your answer to "Who am I?" is the outermost of the many layers of identity reaching inward to the real you. It is one of the significant differences between you and, let's say, a rose, which is named but does not know it. Yet it is one of the things a little girl grows up knowing she will be expected to lose if she marries.

The loss of women's last names may seem compensated for by a custom in first-naming that allows girls to be called by a version of their fathers' names, so that—after a fashion, at least—continuity is restored. In this post-Freudian age it would be bad form to give a boy a version of his mother's first name. Nevertheless, if a couple named Henrietta and Frank should decide to call their son Henry, chances are an earlier Henry, after whom Henrietta was named, provides the necessary male for him to identify with. In any case, the name has come back into its own; it stands foursquare and solid, which is seldom true of the derivative names given to girls. The strength of John is preserved in Joan and Jean, but these are exceptions. Names like Georgette and Georgina, Josephine, Paulette and Pauline, beautiful as they may sound, are diminutives. They are copies, not originals, and like so many other words applied to women, they can be diminishing.

A man in most Western societies can not only keep his name for his lifetime but he can pass it on intact to his son, who in turn can pass it on to *his* son. The use of a surname as a given name is also usually reserved for males, presumably on the grounds that such names do not have a sufficiently "feminine" sound for the "weaker sex." When tradition permits the giving of a family surname to daughters, as in the

American South, a woman can at least retain her identification with that branch of her family. Once a surname has gained popularity as a girl's name, however, it is likely to face extinction as a boy's name. Shirley, for example, an old Yorkshire family name meaning "shire meadow," was once given as a first name only to boys. Not until Charlotte Brontë wrote *Shirley*—a novel published in 1849, whose central character, Shirley Keeldar, was modeled on Charlotte's sister Emily—was it used for a girl.[6] Since then, Shirley has become popular as a girl's name but has dropped out of use as a boy's. Names like Leslie, Beverly, Evelyn, and Sidney may be traveling the same route. Once they have become popular as women's names, their histories as surnames are forgotten, and before long they may be given to girls exclusively.

In English, names like Charity, Constance, Patience, Faith, Hope, Prudence, and Honor no longer have popular equivalents for males, as they often do in other languages. The qualities described are not limited to females, of course, and yet to name a son Honor or Charity, even if doing so breaks no objective rule, would somehow run counter to social expectations. This may be true in part because such names are subjective, expressing more intimately than would seem appropriate for a boy the parents' expectations for their offspring. Or the principle that applied in the case of Shirley may apply here, for once a name or a word becomes associated with women, it is rarely again considered suitable for men.

One of the most useful functions of a given name is to serve as a quick identifier of sex. Nearly everyone, whether they admit it or not, is interested in knowing what sex an unknown person is. You get a postcard from a friend saying he will be stopping by to see you next week with someone named Lee, and chances are the first question that pops into your mind is not whether Lee is young or old, black or white, clever or dull, but whether Lee will turn out to be female or male. Still, natural curiosity does not entirely explain the annoyance or embarrassment some people seem to feel when women have names that are not specifically female by tradition or why names that become associated with women are thenceforth out of bounds for men.

If quick sex identification were the only consideration, the long male tradition of using initials in place of first names would not have come about. People with names like J. P. Morgan, P. T. Barnum, and L. L. Bean were always male—or were they? No one could stop women from sneaking under the flap of *that* tent, and in fact so many did that the practice had to be disallowed. In the early years of this century Columbia University, which in its academic bulletins identified male faculty members only by their surnames and initials, wrote out the names of women faculty members in full—lest anyone unintentionally enroll in a course taught by a woman.[7]

Perhaps it is because of the transience of women's last names that their first names seem often to be considered the logical, appropriate, or even polite counterpart of men's surnames, and the news media frequently reflect this feeling. When Secretary of State Henry Kissinger and Nancy Maginnis were married, many news stories called them "Kissinger and Nancy" after the first paragraph. The usage is so accepted, and its belittling implications so subliminal, that it often persists in defiance of changes taking place all about it. In a magazine story on the atypical career choices of six graduate students, the subhead read "Stereotypes fade as men and women students . . . prepare to enter fields previously dominated almost exclusively by the opposite sex." Three women going into dentistry, business administration, and law were introduced by their full names, as were three men whose fields of study were nursing, library science, and primary education. The men were then referred to as Groves, White, and Fondow, while the women became Fran, Carol, and Pam.[8]

Children, servants, and other presumed inferiors are apt

to be first-named by adults and employers and by anyone else who is older, richer, or otherwise assumed to be superior. In turn, those in the first category are expected to address those in the second by their last names prefixed with an appropriate social or professional title. People on a fairly equal footing, however, either first-name each other or by mutual if unspoken agreement use a more formal mode of address.

As it happens, even though the average full-time working woman in the United States is slightly older than the average man who is employed full-time, she makes only about two-thirds the salary he makes.[9] This may explain why a great many more women than men are called by their first names on the job and why, in offices where most of the senior and junior executives are men and most of the secretaries and clerks are women, the first-naming of all women—including executives, if any—easily becomes habitual. Or it could be that women are at least slightly less impressed by the thought of their own importance, slightly more inclined to meet their colleagues and employees on equal terms. When a reporter asked Ella Grasso, who had just been elected governor of Connecticut, what she wanted to be called and she answered, "People usually call me Ella," a new benchmark for informality must have been set in the other forty-nine state capitals. Unless men respond in the same spirit, however, without taking advantage of what is essentially an act of generosity, women like Governor Grasso will have made a useless sacrifice, jeopardizing both their identity and their prestige.

In the whole name game, it is society's sanction of patronymy that most diminishes the importance of women's names—and that sanction is social only, not legal. In the United States no state except Hawaii legally requires a woman to take her husband's name when she marries, although social pressures in the other states are almost as compelling.[10] The very fact that until recently few women giving up their names realized they were not required to do so shows how universal the expectation is. Any married couple who agree that the wife will keep her own name are in for harassment, no matter how legal their stand: family, friends, the Internal Revenue Service, state and local agencies like motor vehicle departments and voter registrars, hotels, credit agencies, insurance companies are all apt to exert pressure on them to conform. One judge is quoted as saying to a married woman who wanted to revert to her birth name, "If you didn't want his name, why did you get married? Why didn't you live with him instead?"[11] To thus equate marriage with the desire of some women to be called "Mrs." and the desire of some men to have "a Mrs." is insulting to both sexes; yet the equation is so widely accepted that few young people growing up in Western societies think in any different terms.

The judge just quoted was, in effect, defining what a family is in a patronymical society like ours where only males are assured permanent surnames they can pass on to their children. Women are said to "marry into" families, and families are said to "die out" if an all-female generation occurs. The word *family,* which comes from the Latin *famulus,* meaning a servant or slave, is itself a reminder that wives and children, along with servants, were historically part of a man's property. When black Americans discard the names of the slaveholders who owned their forebears, they are consciously disassociating their sense of identity from the property status in which their ancestors were held. To adopt an African name is one way of identifying with freedom and eradicating a link to bondage. The lot of married women in Western society today can hardly be called bondage, but to the degree that people's names are a part of themselves, giving them up, no matter how willingly, is tantamount to giving up some part of personal, legal, and social autonomy.

Since a surname defines a family and identifies its members, a man who marries and has children extends his family, but a woman in marrying gives up her "own" family and joins in extending another's She may be fully aware that she brings to her new family—to her children and grandchildren—the genetic and cultural heritage of her parents and grandparents, but the lineages she can trace are ultimately paternal. Anyone who decides to look up their ancestors through marriage and birth records in town halls and genealogical societies may find paternal lines going back ten or fifteen generations or more, whereas with few exceptions maternal ones end after two or three. The exceptions are interesting for they emphasize how important the lost information from maternal lines really is. Stephen Birmingham, writing about America's blue-blooded families, notes that " 'Who is she?' as a question may mean, 'What was her maiden name?' It may also mean what was her mother's maiden name, and what was her grandmother's maiden name, and so on."[12] Blue bloods, in other words, care a lot about "maiden names," and rightly so, considering that the inputs of maternal genes and culture have as great an effect on offspring as paternal inputs.

Obviously we all have as many female ancestors as male ancestors, but maternal lineages, marked with name changes in every generation, are far more difficult to trace. To most of us the identity of our mother's mother's mother's mother, and that of *her* mother, and on back, is lost forever. How is one affected by this fading out of female ancestors whose names have disappeared from memory and the genealogical records? Research on the subject is not readily available, if it exists at all, but it seems likely that daughters are affected somewhat differently from sons. If it is emotionally healthy, as psychologists believe, for a child to identify with the parent of the same sex, would it not also be healthy for a child to identify with ancestors of the same sex?

A boy, knowing he comes from a long line of males bearing the name Wheelwright, for example, can identify with his forefathers: Johnny Wheelwright in the 1970s, if he wants to, can imagine some medieval John in whose workshop the finest wheels in the land were fashioned, a John who had a son, who had a son, who had a son, until at last Johnny Wheelwright himself was born. No line of identifiable foremothers stretches back into the past to which his sister Mary can lay claim. Like Johnny, she is a Wheelwright, assigned by patronymy to descent from males. What neither boy nor girl will ever be able to trace is their equally direct descent from, let's say, a woman known as the Healer, a woman whose daughter's daughter's daughter, through the generations, passed on the skilled hands which both John and Mary may have inherited.

Imagine, in contrast to Johnny Wheelwright, a hypothetical woman of today whose name is Elizabeth Jones. If you were to ask, in the manner of a blue blood, "Who is she?" you might be told, "She was a Fliegendorf. Her people were Pennsylvania Dutch farmers who came over from Schleswig-Holstein in the seventeenth century." Actually, that tells a fraction of the story. This hypothetical Elizabeth Jones's mother—who met her father at an Army post during the Second World War—was a Woslewski whose father emigrated from Poland as a boy, lived in Chicago, and there married a Quinn whose mother came from Canada and was a Vallière. The mother of that Vallière was the great-great-granddaughter of a woman whose given name was the equivalent of "Deep Water" and who belonged to a group of native North Americans called the Têtes de Boule by French explorers.

Elizabeth Jones's father's mother, in Pennsylvania, had been a Bruhofer, whose mother had been a Gruber, whose mother, a Powel, was born in Georgia and was the great-great-granddaughter of a woman brought to this country from Africa in the hold of a slave ship.

Thus, although Elizabeth Jones is said to have been a Fliegendorf whose people came from Schleswig-Holstein in the sixteen hundreds, fewer than 5 percent of her two thousand or so direct ancestors who were alive in that century had any connection with Schleswig-Holstein, and only one of those who made the passage to America was born with the name Fliegendorf. The same may be said, of course, of Elizabeth Jones's brother Ed Fliegendorf's relationship to the Fliegendorf family or of Johnny Wheelwright's relationship to the bearers of his name. Yet so strong is our identification with the name we inherit at birth that we tend to forget both the rich ethnic mix most of us carry in our genes and the arbitrary definition of "family" that ultimately links us only to the male line of descent.

This concept of family is one of the reasons why most societies through most of history have placed greater value on the birth of a male child than of a female child. Ours is no exception. A survey reported in *Psychology Today* showed that a higher percentage of prospective parents in the United States would prefer to have a son than a daughter as a first or only child. The percentage who felt that way, however, had dropped from what it was only twenty years earlier.[13] Responding to the report, a reader expressed his opinion that the change could be attributed to "a breakdown in the home-and-family ideal" among young parents today. "The son," he wrote in a letter to the editor, "and in particular the eldest son, is strongly tied to the archetypal family; first as its prime agent of continuation, and also as the future guardian and master of the home."[14] Here, then, family and name are seen as synonymous, the male is the prime if not only progenitor, and even the order of birth among male children affects the model of an ideal family.

One could not ask for a better example of how patronymy reinforces the powerful myth that pervades the rest of our language—the myth that the human race is essentially male. The obvious first reaction to such a statement may be to say, "But that's absurd. No one thinks of the race as essentially male." And yet we do. As the social critic Elizabeth Janeway has pointed out, a myth does not really describe a situation; rather, it tries to bring about what it declares to exist.[15]

A childless couple adopted a baby girl. When asked why they chose a girl rather than a boy, they explained that if she did not live up to their expectations because of her genetic heritage, "at least she won't carry on the family." Journalist Mike McGrady states the myth of racial maleness even more tellingly in an article about sperm banking: "One customer . . . gave a reason for depositing sperm that may foreshadow the future: it was to carry on the family line should his male offspring prove sterile. What we are talking about here," McGrady said, "is not fertility insurance but immortality insurance."[16] This customer, then, believes he cannot be linked to future generations through his female offspring, should they prove fertile. His immortality, one must conclude, is not in his sperm or his genes but in his name.

"One's name and a strong devotion to it," wrote an Austrian philosopher, Otto Weininger, around the turn of the century, "are even more dependent on personality than is the sense of property. . . . Women are not bound to their names with any strong bond. When they marry they give up their own name and assume that of their husband without any sense of loss. . . . The fundamental namelessness of the woman is simply a sign of her undifferentiated personality."[17] Weininger, whose book *Sex and Character* had a brief but powerful influence on popular psychology, is of historical interest because he articulated the myth of humanity's maleness at a time when the first wave of feminism was beginning to be taken seriously by governments, trade unions, and other institutions in England and the United States as well as in Europe. In describing the "fundamental namelessness" of woman as "a sign of her undifferentiated personality," Weininger was building support for his premise that "women have no existence and no essence . . . no share in ontological reality, no relation to the thing-in-itself, which, in the deepest interpretation, is the absolute, is God."[18]

Otto Weininger was aware of the movement for women's rights and was deeply disturbed by it. He may well have heard of the noted American feminist Lucy Stone, whose decision to keep her birth name when she married Henry Blackwell in 1855 had created consternation on both sides of the Atlantic. An eloquent speaker with a free and fearless spirit, Stone was widely known as an antislavery crusader. After the Civil War her organizing efforts helped secure passage of the Fourteenth Amendment, which extended the vote to freed slaves who were men. She devoted the rest of her long, productive life to the cause of suffrage for women and founded and edited the *Woman's Journal,* for forty-seven years the major weekly newspaper of the women's movement.

It is especially relevant that among Lucy Stone's many important contributions to history she is best known today for her refusal to give up her name. Her explanation, "My name is the symbol of my identity and must not be lost," was a real shocker to anyone who had not considered the possibility that a married woman could have an individual identity—and in the nineteenth century that meant almost everyone. The law did not recognize such a possibility, as the famous English jurist William Blackstone made clear when he summarized the rule of "coverture," influencing both British and American law for well over a hundred years. "By marriage," he wrote, "the husband and wife are one person in the law—that is, the very being or legal existence of the woman is suspended during the marriage. . . ."[19]

The suspended existence of the married woman came to be well symbolized in the total submersion of a wife's identity in her husband's name—preceded by "Mrs." The use of designations like "Mrs. John Jones" does not go back much before 1800. Martha Washington would have been mystified to receive a letter addressed to "Mrs. George Washington," for at that time the written abbreviation *Mrs.*, a social title applied to any adult woman, was used interchangeably with its spelled-out form *mistress* and was probably pronounced the same way. "Mistress George" would have made little sense.

Lucy Stone's example was followed in the late nineteenth and early twentieth centuries by small but increasing numbers of women, mostly professional writers, artists, and scientists. The Lucy Stone League, founded in New York in 1921, was the first organization to help women with the legal and bureaucratic difficulties involved in keeping their names after marriage. Its early leaders included Jane Grant, co-founder with her first husband, Harold Ross, of the *New Yorker* magazine, and journalist Ruth Hale who in 1926 asked rhetorically how men would respond to the suggestion that they give up *their* names. The suggestion does not often arise, but a psychologist recently described the reaction of one husband and father when someone in his family raised the possibility of changing the family name because they didn't like it:

"He suddenly realized that it was a traumatic thing for him to consider giving up his last name," according to Dr. Jack Sawyer of Northwestern University. "He said he'd never realized before that 'only men have real names in our society, women don't.' And it bothered him also that his name should be a matter of such consequence for him. He worried about his professional standing, colleagues trying to contact him—all kinds of things that women face as a matter of course when they get married. Men have accepted the permanency of their names as one of the rights of being male, and it was the first time he realized how much his name was part of his masculine self-image."[20]

Lucy Stone, whose self-image was comfortably female but not feminine, agreed to be known as Mrs. Stone after her marriage. Through this compromise with custom she avoided the somewhat schizophrenic situation many well-known women face when they use their birth names professionally and their husbands' names socially, thus becoming both Miss Somebody and Mrs. Somebody Else. The Pulitzer-prize-winning novelist Jean Stafford once requested that she be "saluted as *Miss* Stafford if the subject at hand has to do with me and my business or as *Mrs.* Liebling if inquiries are being made about my late husband."[21] Miss Stafford also objected to being addressed as "Ms.," a title that Lucy Stone would probably have welcomed had it been used in her time.

During the nearly two centuries in which the use of a distinguishing marital label was rigidly enforced by custom, the labels *Miss* and *Mrs.* tended to become part of women's names, in effect replacing their given names. A boarding school founded by Sarah Porter in Farmington, Connecticut, soon became known as Miss Porter's School. After the actress Minnie Maddern married Harrison Grey Fiske, she became famous as Mrs. Fiske. In the following classroom dialogue, the columnist Ellen Cohn provides a classic example of how the custom works:

> *Question:* Who is credited with discovering radium?
> *Answer* (all together): Madam Curie.
>
> Well, class, the woman (who was indeed married to a man named Pierre Curie) had a first name all her own. From now on let's call her Marie Curie.
>
> *Question:* Can Madam Curie ever be appropriately used?
> *Answer:* Of course. Whenever the inventor of the telephone is called Mr. Bell.[22]

Through the transience and fragmentation that have traditionally characterized women's names, some part of the human female self-image has been sacrificed. It is hardly surprising, therefore, that the second wave of feminist consciousness brought a serious challenge to patronymy and to the assignment of distinguishing marital labels to women. To be named and defined by someone else is to accept an imposed identity—to agree that the way others see us is the way we really are. Naming conventions, like the rest of language, have been shaped to meet the interests of society, and in patriarchal societies the shapers have been men. What is happening now in language seems simply to reflect the fact that, in the words of Dr. Pauli Murray, "women are seeking their own image of themselves nurtured from within rather than imposed from without."[23]

From antiquity, people have recognized the connection between naming and power. The master-subject relationship, which corrupts the master and degrades the subject, is foreshadowed in one of the biblical creation myths when the primal male assumes the right to name his equal, the primal female. The notion that the sexes were created equal and at the same time is not widely accepted. As Dr. Phyllis Trible, who is a theologian and distinguished scholar of ancient Hebrew Scriptures, has demonstrated, however, when the language of the story is examined outside the traditional confines of patriarchal interpretation, the evidence of full equality is inescapable.[24]

There are two stories of creation in Genesis. In the first chapter, "God created man in his own image . . . male and female created he them." In the second chapter, "God formed man of the dust of the ground" and later made woman from man's rib. Scholars recognize the latter as being the earlier version, and at first glance it seems to reflect a more primitive concept of human beginnings. But closer examination of the older story as it was recorded in the original Hebrew reveals some significant aspects of this ancient human view of ourselves that have been lost in English translations. The "man" formed out of the dust of the ground, Professor Trible points out, is *'adham,* a generic term in ancient Hebrew for humankind. This original person is seen in the story as an androgynous being having the potentialities of both sexes. It is for the protohuman *'adham* that God plans to make a "help meet." (Even in the English of the King James

Version, the adjective "meet" is not the noun "mate," as some people seem to think. "Helpmate" came into the language through what linguists call folk etymology, that is, a change in a word to make it look or sound like more familiar words, without regard to similarity in meaning. A "help meet" is a "fit helper"; a modern translation, the New English Bible, uses the word *partner.*)

In carrying out the plan, God first creates the animals, all of which *'adham* names, thereby asserting authority over them and subjecting them to the service of humanity. The animals are helpers, but because they are not *'adham*'s equals, they are not fit to be full partners. So God tries again by performing surgery on the sleeping androgynous *'adham.*

Up until this time, Trible notes, the ancient Hebrew storyteller consistently used the generic term *'adham.* Only after the rib episode are the Hebrew words specifying the human male, *'ish,* and the human female, *'ishshah,* introduced. *'Adham,* whose flesh and bones have now been sexually identified as female and male, speaks of the two sexes in the third person. "She shall be called woman (*'ishshah*), because she was *differentiated from* man (*'ish*)" provides a valid alternative for the Hebrew term usually rendered "taken out of."

In this ancient Hebrew story, "She shall be called woman" does not represent an act of naming, Trible points out. The typical formula the storyteller uses for naming is the verb *to call* coupled with the explicit object *name.* It is only later—when God has already judged the woman and man but has not yet sent them from the Garden—that the man, invoking the same formula used in naming the animals and asserting supremacy over them, "called his wife's name Eve." Trible concludes, "The naming itself faults the man for corrupting a relationship of mutuality and equality," and God then evicts the primal couple from Eden.

The recorder of that early human effort to understand the nature and meaning of existence speaks across the millenniums of patriarchy. The story is far different from the male-oriented interpretation of creation that has embedded itself in our conscious understanding and our less conscious use of language. In English the once truly generic word *man* has come to mean "male," so that males are seen as representing the species in a way females are not. Humanity divided against itself becomes the norm and the deviation, the namer and the named.

Chapter 2

Who Is Man?

"The Ascent of Man," Jacob Bronowski's acclaimed BBC television series on the evolution of human culture, opens with a program in which the significance of physical adaptation in early hominids is spun in lyric sequence to that watershed of human self-perception, the cave paintings of the Paleolithic period. The series as a whole is remarkable for its stunning and wide-ranging visuals. In this first program two particularly memorable sequences are used to illustrate musculoskeletal development in the only surviving hominid species: scenes of an adult male athlete running and pole-vaulting and poetically executed dissolve shots of a male baby crawling and raising himself to a standing position. The visualizations provide dramatic support for Dr. Bronowski's superb commentary on our beginnings as "man."

To follow the advice of a Bronowski aphorism—ask an impertinent question and you are on the way to a pertinent answer—why did the creators of the program not show either a female athlete or a female baby? If it occurred to them that including a female would provide a more complete and so more accurate image of the human race, why did they reject the idea? Did they feel, consciously or otherwise, that artistic harmony would somehow be compromised if the descriptions of "man" were matched with pictures of a person clearly not a man? They could scarcely have intended to convey the message that males alone participated in the evolution of humankind, yet through the use of imagery limited to males they effectively negated an inclusive, generic interpretation of their title subject.

In choosing the male to represent the norm, Bronowski and his colleagues were following a long-standing tradition in science. What is remarkable is that the habit persists today. In the 1950s, before the rise of black consciousness among whites in the United States, museum exhibits and textbooks on human evolution often showed a series of male figures or faces on an ascending scale with a Caucasian at the top, a black African one step below. The racist misinformation such graphs conveyed is exceeded in its arrogance only by the total exclusion of women from the human race.

The failure of the BBC epic either to conceive or to convey a generic interpretation of *man* in that opening program was confirmed by two additional circumstances. One was the treatment of a particularly important fossil skull as an anomaly: it was identified several times as "the skull of an adult female," although other skulls shown were not identified in terms of sex (the subject under discussion was man, of course). The second and stronger evidence emerged in an interview at the end of the hour-long program when, after a climax marked by homage to the cave painters, the host of the series chatted for a few minutes with a guest anthropologist about what women were doing during this early period in the ascent of man.

The use of *man* to include both women and men may be grammatically "correct," but it is constantly in conflict with the more common use of *man* as distinguished from *woman.* This ambiguity renders *man* virtually unusable in what was once its generic sense—a sense all-too-accurately illustrated in Tennyson's line, "Woman is the lesser man." When Dr. Bronowski said that for years he had been fascinated by "the way in which man's ideas express what is essentially human in his nature,"[1] it is anybody's guess whether his vision included all the anonymous women of the past whose ideas and contributions to science and the arts are no less real for never having been identified.

The newspaper headline THREE-CENT PILL LAST HOPE OF MAN suggests that the story to follow may be an announcement by zero-population-growth researchers of a major contraceptive breakthrough, but actually the news item under that particular headline concerned the personal plight of a fifty-one-year-old Wichita, Kansas, man whose only chance for survival was an inexpensive drug called guanidine.[2] Examples of such ambiguity are endless, and the confusion they cause increases as women come to be seen less as the second sex and more as beings who are fully and essentially human.

Most dictionaries give two standard definitions of *man:* a human being, a male human being. A high school student, thinking about these two meanings, may well ask the obvious question, "How can the same word include women in one definition and exclude them in another?" At which point the teacher may dredge up the hoary platitude, "Man embraces woman"—which gets a laugh but leaves the question unanswered. And the student, perhaps distracted now by continuing snickers, may feel the question is too trivial (and somehow, if she is a girl, too demeaning) to pursue.

In 1972 two sociologists at Drake University, Joseph Schneider and Sally Hacker, decided to test the hypothesis that *man* is generally understood to embrace *woman.* Some three hundred college students were asked to select from magazines and newspapers a variety of pictures that would appropriately illustrate the different chapters of a sociology textbook being prepared for publication. Half the students were assigned chapter headings like "Social Man," "Industrial Man," and "Political Man." The other half were given different but corresponding headings like "Society," "Industrial Life," and "Political Behavior." Analysis of the pictures selected revealed that in the minds of students of both sexes use of the word *man* evoked, to a statistically significant degree, images of males only, filtering out recognition of women's participation in these major areas of life, whereas the corresponding headings without *man* evoked images of both males and females.[3] In some instances the differences reached magnitudes of 30 to 40 percent. The authors concluded, "This is rather convincing evidence that when you use the word man generically, people do tend to think male, and tend not to think female."[4]

The nature of the pictures chosen was interesting in another way, for they demonstrated that *man* calls up largely negative images of power and dominance. The originators of the research project describe the data gathered at their own university (the largest of three samples studied) as follows:

> When we said "Urban Man," as opposed to "Urban Life," students tended to give us pictures portraying sophisticated, upper middle class white males and their artifacts—stereos, cars, bachelor apartments, and so on. We also got pictures of disorganization, slums, demolition. The title "Urban Life" also stimulated pictures of ghettos, but in addition there existed a minor theme of hope—people in the park, building construction, and the like.
>
> When we said "Industrial Man" students gave us pictures of heavy, fairly clumsy machinery, and men doing heavy, dirty, or greasy work. We also got the industrial workers' boss—the capitalist, or corporate executive (e.g., of Mack Trucks, Inc., standing in front of a line of his products). When we said "Industrial Life," we more often received pictures of inside craft work, or of scientific-tech-

nical work—people operating precision optical instruments, oil refineries, etc.—and more pictures of machines without people.

"Economic Man" primarily yielded pictures of disorganization; people at the mercy of the economic system (cartoons of governmental corruption and waste, white collar crime, shots of unemployed workers, small businesses going bankrupt, store window signs indicating rising prices, etc.). A secondary theme was extravagant consumption of the very wealthy, or again, corporate executives, capitalists. The title "Economic Behavior" also stimulated pictures of disorganization and despair, but they tended toward abstract representation of the economic system in trouble, such as graphs, charts, and so on. But "Economic Behavior" appeared to elicit fewer pictures of capitalists than did the term "Economic Man."

"Political Man" was portrayed by pictures of Nixon or other politicians making speeches to mixed audiences. "Political Behavior" was represented by prominent political figures also, but contained a secondary theme of people, including women and minority males, in political protest situations.

"Social Man" was portrayed as a sophisticated white, party-going male (a third to half of the pictures included consumption of alcohol), usually with women around. "Society" involved scenes of disruption and protest, with a subtheme of cooperation among people—kids of various ethnic origins walking in the woods, for example. . . .

When normative white male behavior is portrayed, it is supposed to be cool, sophisticated, powerful, sometimes muscular, almost always exploitive—(getting more than their fair share). A sort of Norman Mailer ideal self is evoked by the use of the word "man." "Behavior" and "life," however, seem to evoke more comprehensively human imagery when people are portrayed. As the image of capitalist, playboy, and hard hat are called forth by the word "man," so it is the other side of the coin called forth by "behavior" or "life"—women, children, minorities, dissent and protest.[5]

These were the responses of young adults who knew, presumably, how dictionaries define *man.* What does the word mean to children, especially the very young? In dictionaries for beginning readers the "human being" definition of *man* is rarely included because it does not relate to anything in a very young child's experience.[6] To a toddler, a "man" may be someone who comes to repair the dishwasher, who puts gas in the car, or who appears on the television screen. In the Golden Picture Dictionary for Beginning Readers the full entry for the word is: "Man, men—A boy grows up to be a man. Father and Uncle George are both men."[7] A child may infer from this definition that mother and Aunt Jane are not men. Nobody, least of all a young child, learns the meaning of *man* from a dictionary, but this limited definition does fit the child's experience. A word means what it means not because of what dictionaries say about it, but because most speakers of the language use it with a certain meaning in mind and expect others to use it with the same meaning. If Billy, at age three or four, were to see the "Avon lady" coming up the front walk and say to his mother, "Here comes a man," she would correct him. If at nursery school he were asked to draw a picture of a man and he drew a figure that appeared to be a woman, he might well be carted off to a psychiatrist.

In primary school, however, children begin to encounter *man* and *men* in contexts that include people like mother and Aunt Jane and the Avon lady. And despite a conflict with the meaning they already know, they are expected at this stage to acquire an understanding of the other, so-called generic meaning of *man.*

Little is known about how or to what extent this transition in understanding takes place, but Alleen Pace Nilsen touched on the subject in a 1973 study she conducted at the University of Iowa. Using a picture-selection technique with one hundred children ranging in grade level from nursery school through the seventh grade, Nilsen found that *man* in the sentences "Man must work in order to eat" and "Around the world man is happy" was interpreted by a majority of children of both sexes to mean male people and not to mean female people.[8] A correlative survey of beginning textbooks on prehistoric people, all having the word *man* (or *men*) in the title, suggests a possible reason for the children's response. Nilsen found that in these books illustrations of males outnumbered illustrations of females by eight to one.[9]

Prehistoric people were also the focus of a more extensive study involving some five hundred junior high school students in Michigan in 1974. Designed by Linda Harrison of Western Michigan University, the study was aimed at finding out how the students interpreted different terms used to refer to early human beings. Approximately equal numbers of boys and girls taking science courses were asked to complete a survey (which would not be graded) by drawing their impressions of early people as they were described in seven statements on human activities at the dawn of civilization—the use of tools, cultivation of plants, use of fire for cooking, pottery making, care of infants, and the like. The statements distributed to one group of students were all phrased in terms of "early man," "primitive men," "mankind," and "he." Students in a second group received the same statements rephrased to refer to "early people," "primitive humans," and "they." For a third group all the statements were worded in terms of "men and women" and "they." The students were also asked to label each character they depicted in the acts of cultivating plants, using tools, making pottery, and so forth, with a modern first name. The number of female and male characters drawn by the students in each group were then counted according to the names assigned. (Names that might have applied to either sex were not counted.)

In the group receiving the "man," "men," "mankind," and "he" statements, more students of both sexes drew male figures only than female figures only for every statement except one. The exception related to infant care, but even there 49 percent of the boys and 11 percent of the girls drew males only. Students of both sexes who illustrated the "people" and "humans" statements also tended to draw more males than females. Those who were given statements referring to "men and women" included the greatest number of female characters in their drawings, although here, too, more students of both sexes drew males only than females only.[10]

Harrison, who is a geologist, notes that the male dominance of the students' responses is probably a reflection not only of the language used on the survey but of the language in which human evolution is usually discussed. "The students' apparent impressions that females were not tool users or plant cultivators are not supported by fossil evidence and inferences about our early predecessors drawn from analogies with hunting and gathering cultures today," she wrote. "It seems likely that females contributed at least an equal share in the early development of agriculture, weaving, and pottery, and to the development of tools used in these endeavors—to the development of what is normally thought of as evidence of culture."[11]

Whatever may be known of the contributions females made to early human culture, an effective linguistic barrier prevents the assimilation of that knowledge in our present culture. Studies like those conducted by Harrison, Nilsen, and Schneider and Hacker clearly indicate that *man* in the sense of male so overshadows *man* in the sense of human being as to make the latter use inaccurate and misleading for purposes both of conceptualizing and communicating.

The "generic man" trap, in which "The Ascent of Man" was also caught, operates through every kind of medium whenever the human species is being talked about. Writing in a national magazine, the psychoanalyst Erich Fromm described man's "vital interests" as "life, food, access to females, etc."[12] One may be saddened but not surprised at the statement, "Man is the only primate that commits rape." Although, as commonly understood, it can apply to only half the human population, it is nevertheless semantically acceptable. But "man, being a mammal, breast-feeds his young" is taken as a joke.

Sometimes the ambiguity of *man* is dismissed on the grounds that two different words are involved and that they are homonyms, like a *row* of cabbages and a *row* on the lake. Two words cannot be homonyms, however, if one includes the other as does *man* in the first definition given by the most recent [1990] Webster's Collegiate Dictionary: "A human being, *especially* an adult male human." Since the definers do not explain whom their italicized "especially" omits, one is left to wonder. Women, children, and adolescent males, perhaps? The unabridged Merriam-Webster Third New International Dictionary is more precise: man is "a member of the human race: a human being . . . now usually used of males except in general or indefinite applications. . . ."

The meaning of a homonym, like *row* or *bow* or *pool,* is usually clear from its context, but the overlapping definitions of *man* often make its meaning anything but clear. Can we be sure, without consulting the board of directors of the General Electric Company, what the slogan "Men helping Man" was supposed to convey? Since GE employs a large number of women, it should be a safe bet that both female and male employees were in the slogan writer's mind. Yet an ad for the company that ran during the same period as the slogan seems to tip the scales in the other direction: "As long as man is on earth, he's likely to cause problems. But the men at General Electric will keep trying to find answers."[13] Maybe the article *the* is the limiting factor, but it is hard to picture any of "the men at General Electric" as female men. Once again the conscious intention to describe man the human being has been subverted by the more persistent image of man the male.

If it were not for its ambiguity, *man* would be the shortest and simplest English word to distinguish humankind from all other animal species. The Latin scientific label *Homo sapiens* is long, foreign, and the *sapiens* part of questionable accuracy. But at least *homo*—like the Hebrew *'adham*—has the clear advantage of including both sexes. Its inclusiveness is demonstrated by the presence in Latin of the words *mas* and *vir,* both of which signify a male person only and distinguish him unequivocally from *femina* or *mulier,* Latin words for "woman." Nevertheless, *homo* is sometimes erroneously understood to mean "male person," and semantic confusion runs riot when it is mistakenly thought to occur in *homosexual,* thereby limiting that term to males. (The prefix *homo-,* as in *homosexual, homonym,* and *homogeneous,* comes from the Greek *homos* meaning "same," and its similarity to the Latin *homo* is coincidental.)

To get back to "humankind," the Greek word is *anthropos,* from which come words like *anthropology* and *philanthropy* as well as *misanthropy,* a blanket dislike of everybody regardless of sex. Like Latin and Hebrew, Greek has separate words for the sexes—*aner* for a male person (its stem form is *andr-*), *gune* (or *gyne*) for a female person. So in English *misandry* is the little-known partner of *misogyny;* but when the two Greek roots come together in *androgyny,* they form a word that is beginning to be used to describe the rare and happy human wholeness that counteracts the destructive linguistic polarization of the sexes.

Although they serve many uses in English, the words for humankind borrowed from classical Greek and Latin have not been called on to resolve the ambiguity of *man.* Native English grew out of a Teutonic branch of the Indo-European family of languages that also produced German, Danish, Norwegian, and Swedish. In the ancestor of all these tongues the word *man* meant a human being irrespective of sex or age. That sense survives in the modern derivatives *mensch* in German, *menneske* in Danish and Norwegian, and *människa* in Swedish, all of which can refer to a woman or a man, a girl or a boy.

The language we speak has no counterpart for these words. However, when *man* was first used in English—as *mann* or sometimes *monn*—it too had the prevailing sense of a human being irrespective of sex and age. About the year 1000 the Anglo-Saxon scholar Aelfric wrote, "His mother was a Christian, named Elen, a very full-of-faith man, and extremely pious."[14] The Oxford English Dictionary cites numerous other examples, including a description written in 1325 of a husband and wife as "right rich men" and a statement from a sermon of 1597 that "the Lord had but one pair of men in Paradise."[15]

At one time English also had separate and unambiguous words to distinguish a person by sex: *wif* for a female, *wer* and *carl* for a male. *Mann*—a human being—dropped the second *n* in combined forms like *waepman* and *carlman,* both of which meant an adult male person, and *wifman,* an adult female person. *Wifman* eventually became *woman* (the plural, *women,* retains the original vowel sound in the pronunciation of the first syllable), while *wif* was narrowed in meaning to become *wife.* But *wer* and *waepman, carl* and *carlman* simply became obsolete; they were no longer needed once *man* was used to signify a male—especially. One cannot help but wonder what would have happened to the word that originally meant a human being if females rather than males had dominated the society in which English evolved through its first thousand years. Would *man* still mean a human being, but especially an adult female?

The question underlines the essential absurdity of using the same linguistic symbols for the human race in one breath and for only half of it in the next. Alma Graham, a lexicographer, draws these contrasts: "If a woman is swept off a ship into the water, the cry is 'Man overboard!' If she is killed by a hit-and-run driver, the charge is 'manslaughter.' If she is injured on the job, the coverage is 'workmen's compensation.' But if she arrives at a threshold marked 'Men Only,' she knows the admonition is not intended to bar animals or plants or inanimate objects. It is meant for her."[16]

Alleen Pace Nilsen notes that adults transfer to children their own lack of agreement about when the many compound words like *workman* and *salesman* apply to both sexes and when such compounds are to be used of males only. She offers some examples to illustrate the different levels of acceptability we sense in such words: "My mother's a salesman for Encyclopædia Britannica" and "Susy wants to be chairman of the dance" are acceptable to many people, but not to all, as is evident from the existence of the terms *saleswoman, chairwoman,* and *chairperson.* "Carol Burnett did a one-man show last night" and "Patsy is quite a horseman, isn't she?" are also acceptable, but they draw attention to the discrepancy between the masculine gender term and the subject's sex. "Miss Jones is our mailman" and "Stella Starbuck is KWWL's new weatherman" seem questionable, perhaps because of the newness in relation to women of the activities they describe. "My brother married a spaceman who works for NASA" and "That newsman is in her seventh month of pregnancy" are generally unacceptable.[17]

If adults cannot agree on when a compound of *man* may be a woman, these terms must be doubly confusing to young children, whose understanding of words is limited by their immediate experience. The meaning a child assigns to a word may be quite different from the meaning an adult assumes the child understands. One youngster, for example, when asked to illustrate the incident in the Garden of Eden story where God drives Adam and Eve from the garden, produced a picture of God at the wheel of a pickup truck, with Adam and Eve sitting in the back surrounded by an assortment of flowering plants for their new home. And there is the story of the children who were disappointed to discover that the "dog doctor" was not a dog at all, but an ordinary human being.

It is not really known at what point children begin to come to terms with the dual role the word *man* has acquired or with the generalized use of *he* to mean "either he or she." Certainly the experience is different for boys and girls—ego-enhancing for the former and ego-deflating for the latter. The four-year-old girl who hides her father's reading glasses and waits for a cue line from him to go find them is *not* expecting to hear, "If somebody will find my glasses, I'll give him a big hug." Yet the same child will sooner or later be taught that in such a sentence *him* can also mean *her*.

At a meeting of the Modern Language Association the story was told of twin girls who came home from school in tears one day because the teacher had explained the grammatical rule mandating the use of *he* when the referent is indefinite or unknown.[18] What emotions had reduced them to tears? Anger? Humiliation? A sense of injustice? It is unlikely that any woman can recapture her feelings when the arbitrariness of that rule first struck her consciousness: it happened a long time ago, no doubt, and it was only one among many assignments to secondary status.

In reporting on her work with children, Nilsen provides some insights on the different routes boys and girls travel in accepting the generic use of *he:*

> It is reasonable to conjecture that because of the egocentricity which psychologists describe as a normal developmental stage of all young children, a boy who is accustomed to hearing such words as *he, him,* and *his* used in relationship to himself will feel a closer affinity to these terms than will a young girl who has instead developed an emotional response to *she, her,* and *hers.* . . .
>
> A young boy who is accustomed to hearing himself and his possessions . . . referred to with masculine pronouns has excellent readiness for acquiring the standard formal rules guiding the treatment of gender in English. As he expands his world to include progressively larger circles of environment and acquaintances he simply expands the size of the body of things referred to with masculine pronouns. It's a very natural process for him to learn that every animate

> being not obviously female is treated as masculine. . . . The only unusual requirement is that at some stage in his development he learns to include females in the body of referents.[19]

For a boy, internalizing the generic interpretation of masculine pronouns is part of a continuum. He becomes aware that a symbol that applies to him is reflected throughout the animate world; a link is strengthened between his own sense of being and all other living things. For a young girl, no such continuum exists.

> When she begins to expand her environment, unlike the boy, she does not simply enlarge her set of referents for the pronouns she is already accustomed to. Instead she has to do a reverse switch. . . .[20]

If a girl is not to experience a recurring violation of reality, she must look upon a familiar symbol for herself as something different and apart from the symbol used for animate beings in general. Older children are taught that we use *he* as a grammatical convention. In itself that is a slight to girls, but at least it is one they can come to grips with intellectually. Younger children have no way of knowing that the mouse or the turtle or the crocodile referred to as *he* is not necessarily a male. "Here he comes," says the TV personality of the woolly bear caterpillar as it marches across the screen.[21] "The groundhog won't see his shadow today," the weather forecaster begins. For several years a national brand of oatmeal was packaged in individual servings, each with an animal illustration and an "educational" note meant to appeal to children. For example: "White Tailed Deer. A native of North America, he was the main source of food for early American settlers." "Buffalo. This North American animal roamed the plains in large numbers. He furnished the Indians with food and warm clothing." "Leopard. A member of the cat family, he lives in Africa and Asia. He is a clever hunter."[22] Only ladybugs, cows, hens, and mother animals with their young are predictably called *she.*

The linguistic presumption of maleness is reinforced by the large number of male characters, whether they are human beings or humanized animals, in children's schoolbooks, storybooks, television programs, and comic strips. From Kukla and Ollie to the Cookie Monster, prestigious puppets and fantasized figures all speak with a male voice. And in Scotland, hunters of the Loch Ness monster tried to lure "him" with an artificial female monster.[23] In short, the male is the norm, and the assumption that all creatures are male unless they are known to be female is a natural one for children to make.

Some writers and speakers who recognize the generic masculine pronoun as a perpetuator of the male-is-norm viewpoint are making the effort required to avoid it. Dr. Benjamin Spock, for example, acknowledged, "Like everyone else writing in the child-care field, I have always referred to the baby and child with the pronouns 'he' and 'him.' There is a grammatical excuse, since these pronouns can be used correctly to refer to a girl or woman . . . just as the word 'man' may cover women too in certain contexts. But I now agree with the liberators of women that this is not enough of an excuse. The fact remains that this use of the male pronoun is one of many examples of discrimination, each of which may seem of small consequence in itself but which, when added up, help to keep women at an enormous disadvantage—in employment, in the courts, in the universities, and in conventional social life."[24] A prominent child psychologist, Dr. Lee Salk, comments in the preface to a book written for parents, "An author interested in eliminating sexism from his or her work is immediately confronted with the masculine tradition of the English language. I personally reject the practice of using masculine pronouns to refer to human beings. Accordingly I have freely alternated my references, sometimes using the female gender and sometimes using the male gender."[25]

If pediatricians and child psychologists tend to be especially sensitive to the harm done by exclusionary language, some linguists are sensitive to what they see as a dangerous precedent when the conventional generic use is replaced by wording like Dr. Salk's "his or her work." James D. McCawley, professor of linguistics at the University of Chicago, once argued that the phrase "he or she" is actually more sexist than *he* alone, which, he said, "loses its supposed sexual bias if it is used consistently."[26] In other words, never, never, never qualify the generic pronoun and you will always be understood to include both sexes. "Why not give him or her a subscription to *XYZ* magazine?" asks a promotional letter. A sexist way to word the question, one imagines Professor McCawley advising the advertising agency: "*He or she* does as much to combat sexism as a sign saying 'Negroes admitted' would do to combat racism—it makes women a special category of beings that are left out of the picture unless extra words are added to bring them in explicitly."[27] McCawley's analogy would be relevant if the sign in question were posted by an organization calling itself "The White People." But nobody ever uses *white* to mean both white and black, the way *he* is sometimes used to mean both he and she. Alma Graham makes the problem clear by stating it as a mathematical proposition: "If you have a group half of whose members are A's and half of whose members are B's and if you call the group C, then A's and B's may be equal members of group C. But if you call the group A, there is no way that B's can be equal to A's within it. The A's will always be the rule and the B's will always be the exception—the subgroup, the subspecies, the outsiders."[28]

Admittedly "he or she" is clumsy, and the reasonable argument that it should be alternated with "she or he" makes it still clumsier. Also, by the time any consideration of the pronoun problem gets to this stage, there is usually a large body of opinion to the effect that the whole issue is trivial. Observing that men more often take this view than women, the syndicated columnist Gena Corea has come up with a possible solution. All right, she suggests, "if women think it's important and men don't . . . let's use a pronoun that pleases women. Men don't care what it is as long as it's not clumsy so, from now on, let's use 'she' to refer to the standard human being. The word 'she' includes 'he' so that would be fair. Anyway, we've used 'he' for the past several thousand years and we'll use 'she' for the next few thousand; we're just taking turns."[29]

Men who work in fields where women have traditionally predominated—as nurses, secretaries, and primary school teachers, for example—know exactly how Corea's proposed generic pronoun would affect them: they've tried it and they don't like it. Until a few years ago most publications, writers, and speakers on the subject of primary and secondary education used *she* in referring to teachers. As the proportion of men in the profession increased, so did their annoyance with the generic use of feminine-gender pronouns. By the mid-1960s, according to the journal of the National Education Association, some of the angry young men in teaching were claiming that references to the teacher as "she" were responsible in part for their poor public image and, consequently, in part for their low salaries. One man, speaking on the floor of the National Education Association Representative Assembly, said, "The incorrect and improper use of the English language is a vestige of the nineteenth-century image of the teacher, and conflicts sharply with the vital image we attempt to set forth today. The interests of neither the women nor of the men in our profession are served by grammatical usage which conjures up an anachronistic image of the nineteenth-century schoolmarm."[30]

Here is the male-is-norm argument in a nutshell. Although the custom of referring to elementary and secondary school teachers as "she" arose because most of them were women, it becomes grammatically "incorrect and improper" as soon as men enter the field in more than token numbers. Because the use of *she* excludes men, it conflicts with the "vital image" teachers attempt to project today. Women teachers are still in the majority, but the speaker feels it is neither incorrect nor improper to exclude them linguistically. In fact, he argues, it is proper to do so because the image called up by the pronoun *she* is that of a schoolmarm. To be vital, it appears, a teacher's image must be male.

No "schoolmarm" was responsible for making *man* and *he* the subsuming terms they have become, though female schoolteachers—to their own disadvantage—dutifully taught the usages schoolmasters decreed to be correct. Theodore M. Bernstein and Peter Farb, respected arbiters of usage, also invoke "schoolmarms" when they want to blame someone for what they consider overconservatism. Bernstein calls his scapegoat "Miss Thistlebottom" and Farb calls his "Miss Fiditch." But on the matter of generic singular pronouns, both men defend the rule that says *he* is the only choice.[31] Ethel Strainchamps, who eschews the role of arbiter, calls that "a recent Mr. Fuddydud 'rule' " and cites examples of contrary usage from the Oxford English Dictionary to prove her point.[32]

By and large, however, the "correctness" of using *man* and *he* generically is so firmly established that many people, especially those who deal professionally with English, have difficulty recognizing either the exclusionary power of these words or their failure to communicate reality. In fact the yearning to understand masculine terminology as including both sexes is sometimes so strong that it asserts itself in defiance of literary or historic evidence to the contrary. Of *course* Alexander Pope's admonition, "Know then thyself . . . the proper study of mankind is man," was intended to include women, we say. But the reader to whom these lines were addressed is made more specific by the author's later reference in the same work to "thy dog, thy bottle, and thy wife."

It was Pope's custom to write his philosophical poems in the form of epistles to particular individuals, and *An Essay on Man,* published in 1733, was written to his friend Henry St. John, Lord

Bolingbroke. Today most readers probably infer that the particular is being made general, that the specific man, Bolingbroke, represents generic "man" in the poet's mind. Pope may have thought so too, but that doesn't solve the linguistic problem. In the unlikely event that he had addressed *An Essay on Man* to a woman instead of to a man, would he have made a categorical reference to her dog, her bottle, and her husband? The question is not as frivolous as it sounds, for the issue is essentially one of categories and what they are understood to include or omit. Women—and in this case wives—are understood to be a category included in generic man. When women are separated from man and grouped with other non-man items like dogs and bottles, the effect on generic man is scarcely noticeable: the subject of the "proper study" remains intact. But if men—and, by extension, husbands—were to be considered a discrete category and were separated from the whole, what would happen to generic man? Would "he" be allowed to consist entirely of women, as he is often allowed to consist entirely of men?

In the spring of 1776, when John Adams and his colleagues in Congress were preparing to dissolve the political bands that connected the thirteen colonies to Great Britain, Abigail Adams wrote to her husband: "In the new code of laws which I suppose it will be necessary for you to make, I desire you would remember the ladies and be more generous and favorable to them than your ancestors. Do not put such unlimited power in the hands of the husbands. Remember, all men would be tyrants if they could. If particular care and attention is not paid to the ladies, we are determined to foment a rebellion, and will not hold ourselves bound by any laws in which we have no voice or representation." Abigail Adams was plainly excluding women from her phrase "all men would be tyrants," for she went on to say, "That your sex are naturally tyrannical is a truth so thoroughly established as to admit of no dispute; but such of you as wish to be happy willingly give up the harsh title of master for the more tender and endearing one of friend."

To which John Adams replied: "As to your extraordinary code of laws, I cannot but laugh. We have been told that our struggle has loosened the bonds of government everywhere; that children and apprentices were disobedient; that schools and colleges were grown turbulent; that Indians slighted their guardians, and Negroes grew insolent to their masters. But your letter was the first intimation that another tribe, more numerous and powerful than all the rest, were grown discontented."[33]

When the Declaration of Independence was issued in Philadelphia a few months later, the self-evident truths that "all men are created equal" and that "governments are instituted among men, deriving their just powers from the consent of the governed," did not apply to women any more than they did to men who were slaves or to those original inhabitants of the country referred to in the document as "the merciless Indian savages."

Lessons in American history provide many more examples of how the part played by women has been distorted or omitted through the use of terminology presumed to be generic. Schoolchildren are taught, for instance, that the early colonists gained valuable experience in self-government. They learn that the Indians, though friendly at first, soon began to plunder the frontier settlements. They are told that pioneers pushed westward, often taking their wives, children, and household goods with them. A child may wonder whether women were involved in the process of self-government or were among the plunderers of frontier settlements, or the child may accept the implication that women were not themselves colonists or Indians or pioneers, but always part of the baggage.

"Man is the highest form of life on earth," the Britannica Junior Encyclopædia explains. "His superior intelligence, combined with certain physical characteristics, have enabled man to achieve things that are impossible for other animals."[34] The response of a male child to this information is likely to be "Wow!"—that of a female child, "Who? Do they mean me too?" Even if the female child understands that, yes, she too is part of man, she must still leap the hurdles of all those other terms that she knows from her experience refer to males only. When she is told that we are all brothers, that the brotherhood of man includes sisters, and that the faith of our fathers is also the faith of our mothers, does she really believe it? How does she internalize these concepts? "We must understand that 'the brotherhood of man' does not exclude our beloved sisters," the eminent scholar Jacques Barzun wrote.[35] But how do we accomplish that feat? By an act of will? By writing it on the blackboard a hundred and fifty times?

The subtle power of linguistic exclusion does not stop in the schoolroom, and it is not limited to words like *man, men, brothers, sons, fathers,* or *forefathers.* It is constantly being extended to words for anyone who is not female by definition. Musing on the nature of politics, for example, a television commentator says, "People won't give up power. They'll give up anything else first—money, home, wife, children—but not power."[36] A sociologist, discussing the correlates of high status, reports that "Americans of higher status have more years of education, more children attending college, less divorce, lower mortality, better dental care, and less chance of having a fat wife."[37] Members of the women's movement in France were arrested for displaying the slogan "One Frenchman in Two Is a Woman"; it was taken by some outraged French males to mean that 50 percent of their number were homosexuals.[38]

If these items appear to be molehills, it must be remembered that the socializing process, that step-by-step path we follow in adapting to the needs of society, is made up of many small experiences that often go unnoticed. Given the male norm, it becomes natural to think of women as an auxiliary and subordinate class, and from there it is an easy jump to see them as a minority or a special-interest group. In 1971, Robert H. Bork, an authority on constitutional law, wrote: "Various kinds of claims are working their way through the judicial system, and the Supreme Court may ultimately have to face them—suits seeking judicial determination of abortion statutes, the death penalty, environmental issues, the rights of women, the Vietnam war."[39] If the Supreme Court is ever asked to make a judicial determination of "the rights of men," it will be a sign that the rights of women and the rights of men have finally become parallel and equal constituents of human rights.

Some authorities, including Professor Barzun, have insisted that *man* is still a universal term clearly understood to mean "person," but the mass of evidence is against that view. As early as 1752, when David Hume referred in his *Political Discourses* to "all men, male and female," the word had to be qualified if it was not to be misunderstood. Dr. Richard P. Goldwater, a psychotherapist, goes to the heart of the matter when he asks, "If we take on its merits [the] assertion that *man* in its deepest origin of meaning stands for both sexes of our race, then how did it come to mean *male*? Did we males appropriate *man* for ourselves at the expense of the self-esteem of our sisters? Did what we now call 'sexism' alter the flow of language through us?"[40]

Those who have grown up with a language that tells them they are at the same time men and not men are faced with ambivalence—not about their sex, but about their status as human beings. For the question "Who is man?" it seems, is a political one, and the very ambiguity of the word is what makes it a useful tool for those who have a stake in maintaining the status quo.

Chapter 3

SEX AND GENDER

During the Second World War a youngster who had been evacuated from London to the country during the blitz wrote an essay on the subject "Birds and Beasts":

> The cow is a mammal. It has six sides, right and left and upper and below. At the back it has a tail on which hangs a brush. With this he sends flies away so they don't fall into the milk. The head is for the purpose of growing horns and so his mouth can be somewhere. The horns are to butt with and the mouth to moo with.
>
> Under the cow hangs milk. It is arranged for milking. When people milk, milk comes and there never is an end to the supply. How the cow does it I have not yet realized, but it makes more and more. The cow has a fine sense of smell and one can smell it far away. This is the reason for fresh air in the country.
>
> A man cow is called an ox. The ox is not a mammal. The cow does not eat much but what it eats it eats twice so that it gets enough. When it is hungry it moos and when it

says nothing at all it is because its insides are full up with grass.[1]

This triumph of logic says two things about what English, as we customarily use it, communicates to children. First, "the linguistic feeling . . . that all creatures are male until proven female" is developed early and firmly, as Alleen Pace Nilsen discovered in her studies at the University of Iowa.[2] Among other things, Nilsen found that both girls and boys have a marked tendency when speaking of animals to use *he* or *it* (often shifting from one to the other) but to avoid *she.* Second, if even a sneaking suspicion exists that an animal might be female, then similar male animals are assumed to belong to some other class. Such a suspicion occurred to the author of "Birds and Beasts," as the reference to a "man cow" makes clear. Therefore, taxonomy to the contrary, since "The cow is a mammal. . . . The ox is not a mammal."

How English conveys such messages is tied up with the grammatical rules that govern gender or, more particularly, with some exceptions to those rules. Gender is simpler in modern English than in other languages. In the first place it is "natural," that is, its three categories—feminine, masculine, and neuter—are assigned, respectively, to female creatures, male creatures, and things that have no sex; and, second, words like *child, teacher, director, president,* which can apply to either of the sexes, are said to have "common gender"—common in the sense of being open to all rather than exclusive.

As linguists use the term, *gender* can be defined as a characteristic of a word that requires other words to agree with it. This is a messy situation in languages that have lots of genders—some as many as ten or eleven, based on things like shape, social rank, and animate or inanimate condition, as well as sex—especially when all modifying words like adjectives, participles, and pronouns have to change their forms to match the words they modify. In modern English, fortunately, pronouns are almost the only modifying words that operate this way. Mary's bicycle is referred to as "hers," John's bicycle as "his," but in both cases the bicycle's parts are "its" wheels, spokes, gears, brakes, and so forth.

Gender in French, German, and other European languages is also classified by sex, but in these languages, unlike English, gender is "grammatical," which is to say that masculine and feminine genders are assigned to inanimate objects as well as to living things. Furthermore, not only pronouns change their forms but other modifying words like articles and adjectives do too. In French "the" is *la* one minute and *le* the next, depending on whether the noun it precedes is feminine or masculine. "La plume de ma tante" remains "la plume" even if my aunt gives it to her husband—not because the pen used to belong to a woman, but because *plume* is a feminine noun and requires a feminine article. If my uncle then loses his pen, the French say "Mon oncle a perdu sa plume," or, as it might seem to an English-speaking person unfamiliar with grammatical gender, "My uncle lost her pen." As people who speak any of the modern European languages know, *why* something is one gender rather than another follows no discernible rules: the German word *mensch,* which means a human being of either sex, is masculine; its Swedish counterpart *människa* is feminine; and in both Danish and Norwegian the equivalent *menneska* is neuter.

Mark Twain once expressed his exasperation with grammatical gender in an essay he called "The Awful German Language," part of which goes like this:

> In German, a young lady has no sex, while a turnip has. Think what overwrought reverence that shows for the turnip, and what callous disrespect for the girl. See how it looks in print—I translate this from a conversation in one of the best of the German Sunday-school books:
>
> "*Gretchen.*—Wilhelm, where is the turnip?
>
> "*Wilhelm.*—She has gone to the kitchen.

"*Gretchen.*—Where is the accomplished and beautiful English maiden?

"*Wilhelm.*—It has gone to the opera."

And Mark Twain went on:

To continue with the German genders: a tree is male, its buds are female, its leaves are neuter; horses are sexless, dogs are male, cats are female—tomcats included, of course; a person's mouth, neck, bosom, elbows, fingers, nails, feet, and body are of the male sex, and his head is male or neuter according to the word selected to signify it, and *not* according to the sex of the individual who wears it—for in Germany all the women wear either male heads or sexless ones; a person's nose, lips, shoulders, breast, hands, and toes are of the female sex; and his hair, ears, eyes, chin, legs, knees, heart, and conscience haven't any sex at all. The inventor of the language probably got what he knew about a conscience from hearsay. . . .

In the German it is true that by some oversight of the inventor of the language, a Woman is a female; but a Wife (*Weib*) is not—which is unfortunate. A Wife, here, has no sex; she is neuter; so, according to the grammar, a fish is *he,* his scales are *she,* but a fishwife is neither. To describe a wife as sexless may be called under-description; that is bad enough, but over-description is surely worse. A German speaks of an Englishman as the *Engländer;* to change the sex, he adds *inn,* and that stands for Englishwoman—*Engländerinn.* That seems descriptive enough, but still it is not exact enough for a German; so he precedes the word with that article which indicates that the creature to follow is feminine, and writes it down thus: "*die Engländerinn,*"—which means "the *she-Englishwoman.*" I consider that that person is over-described.

Well, after the student has learned the sex of a great

> number of nouns, he is still in a difficulty, because he finds it impossible to persuade his tongue to refer to things as "*he*" and "*she,*" and "*him*" and "*her,*" which it has been always accustomed to refer to as "*it.*" When he even frames a German sentence in his mind, with the hims and hers in the right places, and then works up his courage to the utterance-point, it is no use—the moment he begins to speak his tongue flies the track and all those labored males and females come out as "its."[3]

To illustrate how German should be read, even to oneself, Mark Twain then provided a story, complete with capitalized nouns according to the German custom, which he called the "Tale of the Fishwife and Its Sad Fate." In this tragedy the poor fishwife is first stuck fast in a mire, then drops "its Basket of Fishes. . . . It opens its Mouth to cry for Help; but if any Sound comes out of him, alas he is drowned by the raging of the Storm. And now a Tomcat has got one of the Fishes and she will surely escape with him. No, she bites off a Fin, she holds her in her Mouth—will she swallow her? No, the Fishwife's brave Mother-dog deserts his Puppies and rescues the Fin—which he eats, himself, as his Reward."

Then terrible events occur, for lightning strikes and the poor fishwife is consumed by fire in a pathetic, piecemeal fashion. First the flame attacks the fishwife's foot, and "she burns him up." Then one by one the flame destroys other parts of the body until finally

> she reaches its Neck—*he* goes; now its Chin—*it* goes; now its Nose—*she* goes. In another Moment, except Help come, the Fishwife will be no more. Time presses—is there none to succor and save? Yes! Joy, joy, with flying Feet the she-Englishwoman comes! But, alas, the generous she-Female is too late: where now is the fated Fishwife? It has ceased from its Sufferings, it has gone to a better Land; all that is

> left of it for its loved Ones to lament over, is this poor smoldering Ash-heap. Ah, woeful, woeful Ash-heap! Let us take him up tenderly, reverently, upon the lowly Shovel, and bear him to his long Rest, with the Prayer that when he rises again it will be in a Realm where he will have one good square responsible Sex, and have it all to himself, instead of having a mangy lot of assorted Sexes scattered all over him in Spots.[4]

The great American master of the ridiculous and the London child writing with unconscious humor about the English countryside some sixty years later share a certain sense of wonder about the apparent illogicalities of nature. Mark Twain's point, of course, was that a language with grammatical gender can make nature seem absurd to an English-speaking person who assumes that gender equals sex. But his own language makes an equally absurd assumption. To Mark Twain a cow was undoubtedly "she," but the inventor of the German language was a "he," the average German was a "he," and so were the reader and the student—a state of affairs as exasperating as the German oddities he lampooned.

Like the child, Mark Twain was a victim of an exception to the following precise and admirable rule:

> A pronoun must be in the same gender as the noun for which it stands or to which it refers. Each of the following pronouns is limited to a single gender:—*he, him, his* (masculine); *she, her, hers* (feminine); *it, its* (neuter).[5]

And the exception?

> When a referent is either of indeterminate sex or both sexes it shall be considered masculine.[6]

Thus it is bad grammar to say that "the author of 'Birds and Beasts'—who did not know for sure that cows are always female—was justified when she referred to the cow as 'he.' " One has to say that "the author of 'Birds and Beasts' was justified when *he* referred to the cow as 'he.' " But who knows whether the child was a girl or a boy? It doesn't matter, grammarians say. Since no one knows, a masculine pronoun is the proper one to use, and the problem is solved by crediting an unknown boy with something an unknown girl may have written. A German of either sex may be a mixed bag of grammatically feminine and masculine parts who deserves to have "one good square responsible sex," as Mark Twain suggested, but members of the sex that has been robbed blind by a grammatical exception that says, "If you don't know, then it's a he," would settle for one good square responsible pronoun of common gender.

Surely English-speaking women are luckier in this regard than women of other Western countries. At least it is usually possible in English to avoid the generic *he* altogether or to alternate *he* and *she* so as to strike a balance, as Dr. Spock has done in every edition of *Baby and Child Care* published since 1976. In addition to pronouns, a "Dr. Spock" in French would have to alternate all modifiers as well, depending on whether it was the boy's turn or the girl's. "Si le petit est malheureux, peut-être il est malade," would do in the first instance, but in the second it would come out, "Si la petite est malheureuse, peut-être elle est malade." Would such drastic measures be tolerated? Why not? The French are used to grammatical mixing and matching. It goes on all the time, and to be reminded that some 50 percent of babies being cared for at any given moment are female is probably no more of a shock to French-speaking parents than it is to their English-speaking counterparts. In fact, for people who speak languages in which the assignment of gender is frequently unrelated to sex, the impact may be much less sexist than are the blatant generic uses of *man* and *he* in English.

The earliest English of which written records exist—Anglo-Saxon, or Old English—had a gender system not unlike modern German. Every noun was masculine, feminine, or neuter, and its gender assignment often bore no relation to the presence or absence of sex. As in the case of the German *weib,* the Old English word for "woman," *wif,* was neuter. The same was true of the Old English *bearn,* meaning "son." The words for "joy," "bread," and "summer" were masculine; those for "strength," "door," and "hand" were feminine. By the time Old English had evolved into Middle English in the twelfth century, these arbitrary gender assignments were breaking down, and within a few hundred years grammatical gender in English gave way entirely to natural gender. A "woman" was now always a "she," a "son" always a "he," and, except in cases of personification, anything without sex was an "it."

Once *woman, mother, father, son, sister, brother,* and similar words were firmly established in their respective sex-gender categories, the so-called agent nouns—terms like *worker* and *leader* which denote the performer of an action and which can usually be used of either sex—moved into the common gender category. The list of such words is very long: *author, actor, sculptor, scholar, lawyer, doctor, plumber, smith, maker, baker, clown, philosopher, minister, scientist, chief, thief, aviator, carpenter, poet, farmer,* and so on and on. These agent nouns are, in their ultimate origins if not in their immediate past histories, both gender-free and sexless. In the course of their journey into modern English they acquired and lost gender, but *sculptor,* for example, comes from the Latin verb meaning "to carve," *doctor* from the verb "to teach," and *scholar* comes by way of the Latin feminine noun *schola,* meaning "learned leisure," from a Greek verb meaning "to have, hold."

The word *author* is a particularly interesting example. It comes, via Middle English *autour* and Old French *autor,* from the Latin masculine form of the agent noun *auctor,* "one that gives increase," which in turn comes from the verb *augere,* "to increase," "to make grow," "to originate." *Augere* itself is thought to come from the Indo-European root *aug-*, "to increase." Nothing in the meanings "to originate," "to make grow," "to increase" can be construed as solely masculine (despite the erroneous biology that for centuries credited males with the exclusive power of procreation). Yet H. W. Fowler, the lexicographer and expert on English usage, rebuked women writers who would not accept the designation *authoress* as he thought they should. "Their view," he said (obviously without consulting them), "is that the female author is to raise herself to the level of the male author by asserting her right to his name."[7] But who is to say that it is his name and not hers?

Fowler spoke with such authority that his *Dictionary of Modern English Usage* has been reprinted many times in one version or another and today remains a standard reference work for authors, editors, and teachers across the English-speaking world. The evidence within language speaks with authority of a different kind, however, and it demonstrates what Fowler either overlooked or chose to ignore: in language there are no absolutes; once societal perceptions change, language follows suit, and even in the process of change it stimulates and prods toward greater change.

The usage Fowler was defending is a cultural product of the male-as-norm syndrome that in Western countries was largely unchallenged by women until the first great wave of feminist consciousness in the nineteenth century. By that time, arbitrarily assigned gender had all but disappeared, although gender tags in the form of feminine endings were still being tacked onto nouns like *actor* and *poet* to designate females. Also, when new words were coined for new occupations a different form for each sex was often adopted—as in *aviatrix, aviator.* Some feminists prized the "feminine designations" because they felt women should be given credit, as women, for their accomplishments. More, however, objected. When every pen, box, hand, foot, and head was assigned gender, it made sense for nouns designating occupations to be given gender to match the sex of the person referred to; but once grammatical gender dropped out of the language there was no further reason to differentiate, on the basis of sex, between two qualified people: a licensed pilot is an aviator; a licensed physician is a doctor; a poet is a poet. (An actor is also an actor, about which more later.)

When *Modern English Usage* was first published in the 1920s, however, Fowler was convinced that "feminines for vocation-words are a special need of the future." He called them "sex-words" and hoped that new coinages like *teacheress* and *singeress* would find acceptance. He pointed out that more and more women were moving into fields once closed to them and added that "everyone knows the inconvenience of being uncertain whether a doctor is a man or a woman."[8] That particular argument must have seemed ironic to the women who finally, after a long battle, were being accepted in small but growing numbers into the medical profession, not to mention the countless others who had previously had no choice but to put up with the so-called "inconvenience" of going to a male doctor whether they wanted to or not.

The notion that agent nouns ending in *-er* and its variants *-ar* and *-or* "belong" to members of the male sex because these suffixes once denoted masculine gender simply has no validity. Gender assignments, even when they begin life matched to the sex of their referents, have a way of switching back and forth as societal images change, and the history of some of the English agent nouns formed with what were once legitimate masculine or feminine suffixes exposes the fallacy of sexual claims to "vocation words."

In Old English, *-er* (or *-ere*) was a masculine-gender suffix used to form agent nouns denoting male persons only, a restriction that is now, according to the authoritative Oxford English Dictionary, "wholly obsolete."[9] A parallel ending, *-ster* (or *-estre*), was used to denote female persons. Thus in Anglo-Saxon England, when women did virtually all the weaving, baking, and sewing, the agent nouns used to refer to the women who did these jobs were (to give them their modern spellings) *webster, baxter,* and *seamster,* respectively. The editors of the OED point out that in northern England—possibly because men began to adopt these trades—the suffix *-ster* soon came to be used indiscriminately with *-er* as an agent-noun ending, irrespective of sex. A spinster might be either a man or a woman who engaged in spinning. In southern England, however, the *-ster* endings continued to designate female agents through most of the period of Middle English, and the suffix appeared in newly coined words for occupations customarily held by women: bellringestre, hordestre (which meant treasurer), huckster (peddler), and brewster (maker of liquors), to name a few. But these important and often lucrative activities were not to remain the exclusive domain of women, and, as in the north, when men took over the jobs they also assumed the job titles.[10] By the fifteenth century the *-ster* suffix, according to the OED, "no longer had an exclusively feminine sense."[11]

Meanwhile, the French influence on English, which had begun with the Norman invasion in the eleventh century, was reaching its peak. Many words like *countess, duchess, princess, lioness, enchantress,* and *sorceress*—along with their masculine counterparts—found their way across the Channel with little change, and in imitation of these French imports the *-ess* suffix began to be attached to native English words to form feminine-gender compounds like *shepherdess* and *goddess.* Also, as the old native female-occupation titles ending in *-ster* were taken over by males, and the need was felt (by males) for different words to label females within the occupations, the *-ess* suffix was ready at hand. The result was that forms like *seamstress* and *songstress* came into being, leaving *seamster* and *songster* to their new male owners. In the Modern English period, from the sixteenth century on, as the OED documents, "the older words ending in *-ster,* so far as they survived, have been regarded as masculines."[12] The only exception is *spinster,* which reverted to being an exclusively female designation—though with an additional, pejorative meaning that has no male equivalent.

By the nineteenth century, no reservation seems to have been felt about assigning to a "woman's job" the once-masculine *-er* ending—provided that *only* women performed the particular job so designated. The word *seamer,* used in the stocking trade, is a case in point. The OED defines this word by quoting the Penny Cyclopedia of 1843 as follows: "There are three classes of operatives . . .: the 'winders' . . .; the 'stockingers'; and the 'seamers,' who make the stockings out of the pieces thus produced. The 'seamers' are women."

The Latin feminine ending *-trix,* which serves a function similar to *-ess,* was involved in the takeover of another activity traditionally performed by women, though in this case the job title itself was unsuitable for use by men. The old word *midwife* was (and still is) a "woman with" another woman giving birth, just as the Latin *obstetrix* was literally "*she* who stands before" to catch the baby as the mother delivers it. When in the eighteenth century male barber-surgeons began to "deliver" babies, they adopted the Latin word to distinguish their technique—which involved the use of forceps—from that of the midwife, who was prevented from using forceps by law.[13] But the Latin ending *-trix* was clearly recognizable in English as a feminine-gender suffix, so the new title was "defeminized" to *obstetrician.*

From all this evidence, it seems safe to draw a few conclusions. Throughout its history, as English made the gradual change from grammatical to natural gender, words denoting occupations or professions could be and from time to time were used for females and males without distinction. But because males are consciously or unconsciously considered the norm, new feminine designations were introduced and accepted whenever the need was felt to assert male prerogatives. As the language itself documents, once certain occupations ceased to be women's work and became trades or vocations in which men predominated, the old feminine-gender words were annexed by men and became appropriate male designations. Then new endings were assigned to women, quite possibly, in Fowler's phrase, to keep a woman from "asserting her right" to a male's name (or his job).

The OED notes that writers of the sixteenth and succeeding centuries formed derivatives ending in *-ess* very freely. "Many of these are now obsolete or little used, the tendency of modern usage being to treat the agent-nouns in *-er,* and the substantives indicating profession or occupation, as of common gender, unless there be some special reason to the contrary."[14]

What could such special reasons be? No one seems to have made a detailed study of what keeps some feminine-ending terms like *waitress* and *actress* in current, if waning, use although so many others have disappeared. Prestige and economics have clearly been factors in the past (it is no accident, for example, that chefs are usually men and cooks women, or that chefs are better paid than cooks), but other considerations are probably involved as well. It has been suggested, for instance, that the serving of food, being a form of nurture, is so essentially "feminine" an act that when it is done by a woman, her sex is an inseparable part of the action. The suggestion has all the earmarks of male fantasy. One might as well argue that the same act performed by a man is symbolic of dragging the slain mastodon to the entrance of the tribal cave and that it is therefore essentially "masculine," but that possibility is never suggested.

In the theater, where men customarily play male roles and women female roles, the *actor-actress* distinction seems at first glance to be as valid and necessary as the *male-female* distinction. In championing feminine designations, H. W. Fowler commented that "if there is one profession in which more than in others the woman is the man's equal it is acting; & the actress is not known to resent the indication of her sex."[15] Here again, Fowler's unconscious assumption of the male norm led him astray. Increasingly, women in the acting profession speak of themselves as actors, and they do so not to avoid indicating their sex but because *actor* is the generic term for a professional in their field. In the United States they belong to Actors Equity, they may have studied at the Actors Studio or performed at the Actors Playhouse, and they are, in every sense, actors. Alma Graham's formula applies: if the group as a whole is called A, and some of its members are called A's and others B's, the B's cannot be full-fledged A's. The distinction between *actor* and *actress* is not a distinction between male and female; it is the difference between the standard and a deviation. Significantly, when women first began to perform on the English stage in the mid-seventeenth century they, too, were called actors; only after some fifty years did the term *actress* begin to be used.[16]

In the case of *alumnus* and *alumna,* women who object to being called by the masculine-gender form seem to be reversing their stand against feminine designations in other cases. The issue is quite different, though, from the tacking-on of *-ess* endings to English words. *Alumna* and *alumnus,* taken over intact from the Latin, are not agent nouns like *waiter* and *actor;* they are, in effect, extended kinship terms like *daughter* and *son* or *brother* and *sister.* They come from the Latin verb *alere,* "to nourish," and they originally meant "nursling" or "foster daughter," "foster son." This kinship quality is strengthened by their association with *alma mater,* which in Latin means "fostering mother." A woman objects to being called an alumnus for the same reason she objects to being called a son or being subsumed under the word *brotherhood.*

Rhoda Jenkins, an alumna of the University of Pennsylvania and a great-granddaughter of Elizabeth Cady Stanton, sparred with representives of her alma mater over this issue for a number of years. Taking strong exception to fund-raising letters that addressed her as "Dear Alumnus," she finally, in desperation, began to return them (without a contribution) to the male president of the university with a covering note beginning "Dear Madam."[17]

The difference between words that legitimately refer to a person's sex (like the kinship terms and such rare sex-dependent agent nouns as *wet nurse* and *sperm donor*) and the suffix words used to introduce an irrelevant sexual distinction is elusive but important. Failure to acknowledge and to respect this difference contributes to the overly rigid separation into "feminine" and "masculine" of characteristics common to both males and females. When grammarians use the word *gender* they know they are referring to a convention that may overlap *sex* or may have nothing to do with it. When psychiatrists use the word *gender* they, too, assign it a specific meaning that can match *sex,* although it does not necessarily do so. At the risk of oversimplification, "sex" in both contexts is a biological given; "gender" is a social acquisition. Yet most people, including most grammarians and psychiatrists, occasionally confuse the two terms, and by using them as though they were synonymous, they semantically blur a biological given with something that is socially induced.

A court case adjudicated in Great Britain in 1971 was based on the distinction between gender and sex. The dispute involved the marriage of a transsexual who was described as having been changed medically from a male to a female. Lawyers argued that since the respondent was treated by society as a woman for many purposes, including the payment of national insurance, "it is illogical to refuse to treat her as a woman for the purpose of marriage." The judge, Mr. Justice Ormrod, disagreed. "The illogicality," he ruled, "would only arise if marriage were substantially similar in character to national insurance and other social situations, but the differences are obviously fundamental." Arguments to the contrary, he said, "confuse sex with gender. Marriage is a relationship which depends on sex and not on gender."[18]

A far better known case is that of Jan Morris, born James Morris, who described in her book *Conundrum* her reasons for wanting to become a woman. To her, gender is more important than sex, and the decision she made to change her body was a matter of changing her sex to fit her gender. "Nobody in the history of humankind has changed from a true man to a true woman, if we class a man or a woman purely by physical concepts," she says. Yet "to me gender is not physical at all. . . . Male and female are sex, masculine and feminine are gender, and though the conceptions obviously overlap, they are far from synonymous."[19]

Jan Morris and Mr. Justice Ormrod may differ as to whether sex or gender is more important, but they agree that the two are not identical. What makes Jan Morris's history cogent is her eloquent testimony to the psychic consequences of overly rigid social stereotyping.

In English "natural gender" means exactly that: if a person is male, masculine pronouns are used to refer to him, and he is called, as appropriate, by masculine-gender words—*son, brother, husband, father, uncle, grandfather.* His primary and secondary sex characteristics are male, but no one has established that the capabilities of his mind are sex-linked. Unless he is a professional sperm donor, no occupation he holds has not at one time or another been held by a woman.

> Rich man, poor man, beggarman, thief,
> Doctor, lawyer, merchant, chief,
> Tinker, tailor, soldier, sailor—

The old counting-out rhyme has a long history of counting out women and girls, but its history is not yet over. *Man* is probably irretrievable as a true generic, but the other words—the agent nouns of daily life—are finally coming into their own as words whose only gender is the common gender of humanity.

Chapter 4

SEMANTIC POLARIZATION

Two statements, one by a professor of linguistics and the other by a professor of psychiatry, explain rather neatly, when looked at together, the part words play in molding cultural assumptions. Dr. Calvert Watkins, the linguist, says, "The lexicon of a language remains the single most effective way of approaching and understanding the culture of its speakers."[1] Dr. Theodore Lidz, the psychiatrist, says, "The form and functions of the family evolve with the culture and subserve the needs of the society of which it is a subsystem. . . . Among the most crucial tasks performed by the family is the inculcation [in children] of a solid foundation in the language of the society."[2] Put together, the statements say: the words we use daily reflect our cultural understandings and at the same time transmit them to the next generation through an agency that subserves the culture's needs.

Dr. Lidz spells out the relationship of language to culture in more detail:

> . . . Language is the means by which people internalize experience, think about it, try out alternatives, conceptual-

ize a future and strive toward future goals. . . . Indeed, the capacity to direct the self into the future, which we shall term "ego functioning," depends upon a person's having verbal symbols with which to construct an internalized symbolic version of the world that can be manipulated in imaginative trial and error before committing himself or herself to irrevocable actions.

To understand the importance of language to ego functioning, we must appreciate that in order for anyone to understand, communicate, and think about the ceaseless flow of experiences, people must be able to divide their experiences into categories. . . . Each child must learn the culture's system of categorizing, not only in order to communicate with others in the society, but also in order to think coherently. Each culture is distinctive in the way in which its members categorize their experiences and its vocabulary is, in essence, the catalogue of the categories into which the culture divides its world and its experiences.[3]

This basic linguistic theory is borne out by anthropological studies of widely diverse cultures throughout the world. The recognition of the relationship of vocabulary to culture was what led to the realization that the way human beings view such things as time and space, color, family relationships, sex, and supernatural beings varies enormously from one society to another. Surprisingly, however, few studies of the dominant culture of present-day America have explored its "categories of experience" by looking at our common vocabulary—the ordinary words that ordinary people speak every day. These are the words of the mass media and popular literature, the currency of basic verbal exchange. They are the building blocks of the language we use continuously to structure thinking and to convey ideas and information. Inevitably, since they are accepted and used within the culture, these everyday words carry a burden of the culture's preconceptions and prejudices.

This is not to say that words themselves are pejorative or oppressive. When a social practice like prostitution exists, there can be no objection to giving it a name. But when such ordinary words for a female person as *woman* and *girl* acquire the additional commonly understood meanings of "mistress" and "prostitute," as Webster's unabridged dictionary attests has happened in English, an attitude toward women held by some members of society becomes part of the experience of all the society's members. When parents or teachers tell a boy not to cry because it isn't "manly" or praise a girl for her "feminine" way of dressing, they are using the words *manly* and *feminine* to reinforce the categories our culture has assigned to males and females. As Calvert Watkins says, language "is at once the expression of culture and a part of it."[4]

Biological differences between females and males are universal and obvious, and every society has used them as a basis on which to assign roles. Role assignment according to sex does not stop with reproductive function, however, but is extended to other areas which vary from one culture to another in seemingly arbitrary ways: in one society, for example, women till the fields and carry heavy burdens, in another men do these tasks. The work of cultural anthropologists has made this kind of information widely available. What the anthropologists also emphasize, although these findings have been less widely popularized, is that the extent to which roles are assigned on the basis of sex and the rigidity with which the sexes are categorized also varies greatly. In some societies, including our own, the importance placed on sexual difference is so great that the existence of normal, temperamental differences occurring within each sex, and found in an equally great range in both sexes, is all but denied. These are the differences that in a less rigid scheme can be fully used for the common good but that in a society like our own tend to be repressed.

What may be new about this old information is the extent to which our common vocabulary contributes to social categorizing. We toss around words like *masculine* and *feminine* as though they described immutable characteristics that everyone will immediately recognize as the "normal" and "proper" endowments of male and female people. In the United States, according to Dr. David Abrahamsen, a psychoanalyst specializing in behavioral disorders, "we have a masculine self-image. I think it's time it was a little more feminized, a little more passive and peaceful. If you have a brain, you are thought to be a sissy. If you have muscles on the football field, you are an American. It's almost un-American to have a brain."[5] It is also almost un-American to question the meanings of "masculine" and "feminized."

These words and others like them are so much a part of the way we perceive ourselves that we tend not to think about how we came to accept them or about their power to mold others in the same matrix. We do not question what the words—whether we want them to or not—are communicating: that qualities like toughness and timidity, openness and guile, integrity, beauty, and courage are sex-related; that "stonewalling it" is a virtue because only a he-man can stand up to pressure; that gentleness leads to weakness and tenderness to softheadedness; that our sex-differentiated cultural categories are in the main male-positive-important on the one hand, female-negative-trivial on the other. If these statements seem exaggerated, a look at a number of words as they are defined in standard American dictionaries shows that they are not.

Webster's Third New International Dictionary (1986) defines *manly,* for example, as "having qualities appropriate to a man: not effeminate or timorous; bold, resolute, open in conduct or bearing." The definition goes on to include "belonging to or appropriate in character to a man" (illustrated by "manly sports" and "beer is a manly drink"), "of undaunted courage: gallant, brave." The same dictionary's definition of *womanly* is less specific, relying heavily on phrases like "marked by qualities characteristic of a woman"; "possessed of the character or behavior befitting a grown woman"; "characteristic of, belonging to, or suitable to women: conforming to or motivated by a woman's nature and attitudes rather than to a man's." Two of the examples provided are more informative: "convinced that drawing was a waste of time, if not downright womanly . . ." and "her usual womanly volubility."

In its definition of *manly* the Random House Dictionary of the English Language (1967) supplies the words "strong, brave, honorable, resolute, virile" as "qualities usually considered desirable in a man" and cites "feminine; weak, cowardly," as antonyms. Its definitions of *womanly* are "like or befitting a woman; feminine; not masculine or girlish" and "in the manner of, or befitting, a woman." The same dictionary's synonym essays for these words are worth quoting in full because of the contrasts they provide:

> MANLY, MANFUL, MANNISH mean possessing the qualities of a man. MANLY implies possession of the most valuable or desirable qualities a man can have, as dignity, honesty, directness, etc., in opposition to servility, insincerity, underhandedness, etc.: *A manly foe is better than a weak friend.* It also connotes courage, strength, and fortitude: *manly determination to face what comes.* MANFUL stresses the reference to courage, strength, and industry: *manful resistance.* MANNISH applies to that which resembles man: *a boy with a mannish voice.* Applied to a woman, the term is derogatory, suggesting the aberrant possession of masculine characteristics: *a mannish girl; a mannish stride.*
>
> WOMANLY, WOMANLIKE, WOMANISH, mean resembling a woman. WOMANLY implies resemblance in appropriate, fitting ways: *womanly decorum, modesty.* WOMANLIKE, a neutral synonym, may suggest mild disapproval or, more rarely, disgust: *Womanlike, she (he) burst into tears.* WOMANISH usually implies an inappropriate resemblance and suggests weakness or effeminacy: *womanish petulance.*

What are these parallel essays saying? That we perceive males in terms of human qualities, females in terms of qualities—often negative—assigned to them as females. The qualities males possess may be good or bad, but those that come to mind when we consider what makes "a man" are positive. Women are defined circularly, through characteristics seen to be appropriate or inappropriate to women—not to human beings. In fact, when women exhibit positive attributes considered typical of men—dignity, honesty, courage, strength, or fortitude—they are thought of as aberrant. A person who is "womanlike" may (although the term is said to be "neutral") prompt a feeling of disgust.

The broad range of positive characteristics used to define males could be used to define females too, of course, but they are not. The characteristics of women—weakness is among the most frequently cited—are something apart. At its entry for *woman* Webster's Third provides this list of "qualities considered distinctive of womanhood": "Gentleness, affection, and domesticity or on the other hand fickleness, superficiality, and folly." Among the "qualities considered distinctive of manhood" listed in the entry for *man,* no negative attributes detract from the "courage, strength, and vigor" the definers associate with males. According to this dictionary, *womanish* means "unsuitable to a man or to a strong character of either sex."

Lexicographers do not make up definitions out of thin air. Their task is to record how words are used, it is not to say how they should be used. The examples they choose to illustrate meanings can therefore be especially revealing of cultural expectations. The American Heritage Dictionary (1969), which provides "manly courage" and "masculine charm," also gives us "Woman is fickle," "brought out the woman in him," "womanly virtue," "feminine allure," "feminine wiles," and "womanish tears." The same dictionary defines *effeminate,* which comes from the Latin *effeminare,* meaning "to make a woman out of," as "having the qualities associated with women; not characteristic of a man; unmanly" and "characterized by softness, weakness, or lack of force; not dynamic or vigorous." For synonyms one is referred to *feminine.*

Brother and *sister* and their derivatives have acquired similar features. A columnist who wrote that "the political operatives known as 'Kennedy men' and 'Nixon men' have been sisters under their skins" could not possibly have called those adversaries "brothers," with all the mutual respect and loyalty that word implies. As the writer explained, "Like the colonel's lady and Judy O'Grady, their styles were different but their unwavering determination to win was strikingly similar."[6] Other kinds of sisters for whom no comparable male siblings exist include the sob sister, the weak sister, and the plain ordinary sissy, whose counterpart in the brotherhood is the buddy, a real pal. Like *effeminate,* these female-related words and phrases are applied to males when a cutting insult is intended.

Masculine, manly, manlike, and other male-associated words used to compliment men are frequently also considered complimentary when applied to women: thus a woman may be said to have manly determination, to have a masculine mind, to take adversity like a man, or to struggle manfully against overwhelming odds. The one male-associated word sometimes used to insult her is *mannish,* which may suggest she is too strong or aggressive to be a true woman, or that she is homosexually oriented, in which case *mannish* can become a code word.

Female-associated words, on the other hand, must be hedged, as in "He has almost feminine intuition," if they are used to describe a man without insulting him. He may be praised for admirable qualities defined as peculiar to women, but he cannot be said to have womanly compassion or womanlike tenderness. In exceptions to this rule—for example, when a medic on the battlefield or a sports figure in some situation of unusual drama is said to be "as gentle as a woman"—the life-and-death quality of the circumstances makes its own ironic and terrible commentary on the standards of "masculinity" ordinarily expected of men.

The role expectations compressed into our male-positive-important and female-negative-trivial words are extremely damaging, as we are beginning to find out. The female stereotypes they convey are obvious, but the harm doesn't stop there. The inflexible demands made on males, which allow neither for variation nor for human frailty, are dehumanizing. They put a premium on a kind of perfection that can be achieved only through strength, courage, industry, and fortitude. These are admirable qualities, but if they are associated only with males, and their opposites are associated only with females, they become sex-related demands that few individuals can fulfill.

A study conducted in the 1950s by the psychologist Ruth E. Hartley revealed some of the burden our male-oriented culture puts on preadolescent boys.[7] The boys Hartley studied saw men as needing to be "strong," "ready to make decisions," and "able to protect women and children in emergencies." Men have to have more manual strength than women, know how to carry heavy things, be able to fix things, and get money to support their families, the boys believed. "[T]hey are the ones to do the hard labor, the rough work, the dirty work, and the unpleasant work. . . . [T]hey also need to know how to take good care of children, how to get along with their wives, and how to teach their children right from wrong."

Girls and women, as might be expected, were described by these boys in terms of a load of negative and limited qualities. Specifically, "Women do things like cooking and washing and sewing because that's all they can do." "If women were to try to do men's jobs, the whole thing would fall apart with the women doing it." "Women haven't enough strength in the head or in the body to do most jobs." "In going to adventurous places women are pests—just a lot of bother. They die easily and they are always worried about their petticoats."

An amusing picture, but the conclusions Hartley reached are anything but funny. For many boys the scramble to escape femininity "takes on all the aspects of panic, and the outward semblance of non-femininity is achieved at a tremendous cost of anxiety and self-alienation." From the results of the study, Hartley inferred that the degree of anxiety a boy experiences has a direct relationship to the degree of pressure exerted on him to be "manly."

Many factors are involved in the conflict these children revealed. Among them Hartley identifies lack of adequate role models, extensive supervision by women, and the rigidity of role demands. She does not specifically mention the effect of semantic categorizing, but her own choice of words in describing the boys' plight suggests its centrality. "On the one hand," she says, "we have insisted that he eschew all 'womanly' things almost from the cradle, and enforced these demands in a way that makes whatever is female a threat to him—for that is what he must not be." Yet society, which tells the male child to disdain "sissies" at all costs, forces him "into close contact with the epitome of all sissy-things—women. . . ."

If, as Theodore Lidz and others maintain, words are "carriers of categories developed by the culture" and language is the means by which we internalize our experience, the polarized meanings of the words we use to describe women and men cannot be ignored. By the age of five, children are already affected by the positive qualities culturally assigned to males and the almost complete absence of positive qualities attributed to females. Hartley cites several research studies of kindergarten children which show that "boys are aware of what is expected of them . . . and restrict their interests and activities to what is suitably 'masculine' in the kindergarten, while girls amble gradually in the direction of 'feminine' patterns for five more years. In other words, more stringent demands are made on boys than on girls and at an early age, when they are least able to understand either the reasons for or the nature of the demands." The reaction of young males is "anxiety which frequently expresses itself in overstraining to be masculine, in virtual panic at being caught doing anything traditionally defined as feminine, and in hostility toward anything even hinting at 'femininity' including females themselves."

No wonder. The women these boys are trying to escape were once little girls whose only challenge was to amble toward femininity. In tragic numbers they have either become ciphers or their rebellion against nonentity has turned them into the overdemanding, overpossessive moms of the caricatures. In some cases the dictionary examples are all too appropriate. For many women it has become natural to cry, to be petulant, to waste time, to be late, to accomplish things through deceitful stratagems, to be domineering, ill-tempered viragoes. No wonder little boys want to run from them and what they seem to stand for, even if doing so blocks their own wellsprings of tenderness and compassion.

And no wonder little girls grow aimlessly. "What woman needs," Margaret Fuller once said, "is not as a woman to act or rule, but as a nature to grow, as an intellect to discern, as a soul to live freely, and unimpeded to unfold such powers as were given her."[8] If she is thought of and defined only as a woman, not as a nature free to develop full human powers, she is doomed to revolve in that unreal circle of what is "characteristic of, belonging to, or suitable to a woman's nature."

In addition to reflexive and negative definitions, many words used to describe females have traveled a road that linguists call degeneration of meaning. The case histories of *virago* and *shrew* are interesting examples. *Virago,* which like *virtue* comes from the Latin *vir* meaning "male person," was once a noble word. It usually designated a woman of exceptional strength and courage, but it was also applied to men with similar qualities. Gradually it ceased to be used of men, perhaps because it signified no more than was expected of them. Today it is applied only to females, and courage has been almost wholly replaced by bad temper and unusually great physical strength or size. *Virtue,* on the other hand, remains a noble word embodying moral excellence, righteousness, and responsibility when applied to people of either sex; a further meaning—chastity—is understood to apply to women only.

Historically, *shrew* starts out differently but ends up with much the same meaning as *virago.* In the thirteenth century a shrew was "a wicked, evil-disposed, or malignant man" and the word was used specifically to refer to the Devil. Applied to males, it weakened gradually in meaning through "rascal" and "villain" until by the nineteenth century it expressed only mild reprobation, as in a reference by Robert Louis Stevenson to "our poor shrew of a parson." The original meaning of the word, however, had been extended by Chaucer's time to include "a person, especially a woman, given to railing or scolding or other perverse or malignant behavior." Once applied to women, this meaning was soon assigned exclusively to them and is the only one that survives.[9]

In general, such changes in the meanings of words according to their sex assignment follow a pattern that might be called semantic polarization. Having acquired a sense that is related more to one sex than the other, words tend to fit into and reinforce the male-positive-important and female-negative-trivial cultural categories. *Master* and *mistress* are striking examples. Both come from the Indo-European root form meaning "great" or "much," and in some contexts both retain a sense of authority over others (though today the others are more likely to be pets than people). In their most common uses, however, *master* now denotes excellence in performance, and *mistress* labels the so-called kept woman. When titles for nobility are given extended applications, their meanings diverge in a similar way. *Queen, dame,* and *madam* have all acquired additional derogatory connotations without counterparts in *king, lord,* and *sir.* A teacher writes of trying to describe one of her most attractive and capable students: "I found myself saying 'She's really a prince.' Appalled as I was at my own pro-masculine description, I just couldn't say that she was a *princess* because *princess* connotes someone who is fussy and spoiled and accustomed to living in the lap of luxury."[10]

The devaluation of words has its uses, of course, and can easily be accomplished by tagging them with feminine-gender suffixes. When Ella Grasso was campaigning in 1974 for the chief executive office of Connecticut, some of her political rivals came up with the slogan "Connecticut doesn't need a governess." Seventy years earlier opponents of suffrage for women employed the ridiculing label "suffragette." The effect of "-ette" is so immediately belittling, in fact, that it is often invoked on the spot—as in *jockette* or *astronette*—to establish a female-negative-trivial category when male prerogatives are threatened.

Tomboy is one of the few words whose meaning was elevated rather than degraded when it came to be used of females only. According to the Oxford English Dictionary the word in its earliest uses meant "a rude, boisterous, or forward boy." An example, "whiskyng and ramping abroade like a Tom boy," dates from 1553. Since then the meaning has changed twice. The first change extended it to females in the sense of "a bold or immodest woman." The OED quotes from a sermon of 1579, "Sainte Paul meaneth that women must not be impudent, they must not be tomboyes, to be shorte, they must not bee unchaste." The quotation illustrates the first thing that customarily happens to a low-value word when it is switched from males to females: it acquires a sense of sexual promiscuity.

This meaning of *tomboy* did not persist, however. Perhaps the aura of full-blown adult female sexuality was incompatible with the sense of sexual inexperience or innocence brought to mind by the word *boy*. In any case, as the male meaning of *tomboy* disappeared and the female meaning dropped in age level, the word lost its connotation of sexiness and began to acquire some of the attractive qualities of *boy*. "What I mean by 'tomboyism,' " wrote the English novelist Charlotte Yonge in 1876, "is a wholesome delight in rushing around at full speed, playing at active games, climbing trees, rowing boats, making dirt-pies, and the like."[11]

That a girl could behave in such a fashion, especially with wholesome delight, was a shockingly new idea in the Anglo-American culture of Yonge's day. Clothes and manners were constricting, and active role models for young girls were almost nonexistent. So were active word models. When the early meaning of *virago* became obsolete and no alternative arose to take its place, the language lost a word that described heroic qualities in women. Even so, *virago* had never been a completely positive word, for in addition to meaning strong and courageous it also meant—as is clear from its derivation—manlike. In other words, a woman was not thought of as heroic in her own right; she had to be likened to a man.

Tomboy is similarly faulted as a word model, and because it is used of children, the psychic damage it inflicts is even greater. A tomboy is "a girl of boyish behavior," according to one dictionary, "a young girl who behaves like a lively, active boy," according to another. But why must a girl be defined in terms of something she is not—namely, a boy? Where is the word that would bring to mind a lively, spirited girl without the subliminal implication of imitation or penis envy? Most girls who like sports and the out-of-doors or who have intellectual or mechanical abilities are not trying to be boys. They are trying to be themselves. To call them tomboys, even with the intention of being complimentary, disparages them for being girls.

In contrast to descriptives like *virago* and *tomboy,* the word *hysterical* is usually used to describe a woman as though she were simply behaving according to expectations. Derived from the Greek word for "womb" (because uterine disturbances were thought to be its cause), *hysteria* now refers in technical use to a specific psychoneurosis that may affect anyone, male or female. In popular usage it is a state of excessive fear or other emotion in individuals or masses of people, but in this sense men—

whether individually or in groups—are seldom said to be hysterical. After a series of rapes at a large state college, news stories repeatedly described a "mood of hysteria" among women students on the campus. The description, according to the dean of women, was totally false. "The mood of the women is one of concern and anger," she told reporters. "When men feel concern and anger, it is called concern and anger, never hysteria."[12] No comment was required on the power of the label to evoke images of hysterical women as potential victims of rape.

Thinking about the word *hysteria,* Juli Loesch speculated on the relationship between the different cultural attitudes toward crying that are instilled in girls and boys, and the roots of violence in the modern world. In reading her comments, one cannot help but be struck by the need for nontechnical and graphic words to describe the sickness that results when the characteristics people persist in labeling "masculine" are pushed to their extremes:

> When girls are comforted and boys ignored or ridiculed when they cry, females often grow up crying whether they want to or not. And males grow up NOT crying—whether they want to or not. This gives men a big power advantage (it's hard for a blubbering woman to appear "mature" and confident vis-à-vis a tight-lipped man) but leaves men with an often painful lack of emotional outlet.
>
> This crippled emotional condition found in males, which I call "testeria" (>testes, L. for balls) accounts in part for the ability of the male ruling class to efficiently, calmly, and maturely carry out planetary catastrophe. Male inventions like war, capitalism, totalitarianism, industrialism, and other atrocities are only possible if millions of efficient, calm, mature male people are diligently repressing their healthy human emotions. Since the turn of the century, over 50 million human beings have been slaughtered in war by psychiatrically normal male people.

Along with testeria—the condition of having puny, inadequate emotional responses—comes another male-linked disease which is even more serviceable to the masculine mystique—penisolence.

Testeria is mostly a matter of repression or reserve: the inability to feel, or to express certain feelings. Penisolence is the *active* phase of male emotional disease. . . . It is a pushy and invasive attempt to master one's own distress by mastering other people.

The "feminine" converse of this behavior—hysteria—complements male powerfreak behavior and allows it to rampage unchallenged. Women who are accustomed to feeling helpless and even physically sick when a crisis hits, can't effectively oppose a tight-lipped testerical male bent on pushing his penisolent way into the world. Men are taught to turn fear and guilt into aggressive action, and women are taught the opposite: to let aggressive impulses dissolve into a queasy emotional stew.

Psychiatry has routinely defined male behavior as a norm and female behavior as an aberration. Thus "hysteria" is listed in psychology textbooks as a disease, while there is no recognition at all of "testeria" as a dangerous pathological condition. . . .

It is certainly true that not all men succumb to testeria to the same extent, and neither are all women subject to hysterical symptoms. But since men use their testeria to oppress women, and since ruling-class penisolence is on the verge of cinderizing the planet, it looks as if a female revolution will be necessary (if not sufficient) to end this madness.[13]

Machismo probably comes closest to Loesch's *testeria* and *penisolence.* It is so new to English that dictionaries published before the seventies did not include it: the qualities it describes were unacknowledged. In its native Mexico (the word comes from the Spanish *macho,* meaning "male") *machismo* is used to compliment men for virility and a sense of pride in themselves as males. It has overtones, however, of excessive concern with "masculinity," and it is this connotation especially that has carried over into English. The definition in the 1973 edition of the American Heritage Dictionary is explicit in this regard: machismo, it says, is "an exaggerated sense of masculinity stressing such attributes as physical courage, virility, domination of women, and aggressiveness or violence."

The value of words like *machismo* and Loesch's neologisms lies in their ability to isolate an aberration of society that needs to be examined. But like all words used to describe characteristics that have, or are thought to have, sexual origins, they are especially subject to abuse as polarizing labels. "The existence in a given society of a dichotomy of social personality," Margaret Mead observed in *Sex and Temperament,* "of a sex-determined, sex-linked personality, penalizes in greater or less degree every individual born within it."[14]

Unfortunately, a cherished and semantically underlined precept of our culture seems to be that the sexes must be thought of as opposite. *Opposite* frequently means "set over against," hostile, opposed. It denies mutuality and equality. The ancient belief that contrasting female and male forces are at work in everything—the yin-yang of dark and light, of passive and active, of negative and positive in inanimate nature as well as in people—too easily becomes an adversary concept. The biological union of female and male is not.

Whether applied to living things or by analogy to objects, the adjectives *female* and *male* are culture-free and explicit. No one needs to consult a manual to find out how female and male electrical parts fit together to form a union, and one part is not considered better or stronger or more important than the other. They work together, and their use is limited to performing a particular function.

Masculine and *feminine* are very different from *male* and *female.* Instead of being specific they are vague and subjective and perhaps the most culturally biased words in the language. Rarely employed in a biological sense, they are used instead to describe what a group or society has decided female and male persons should (or should not) be. As Margaret Mead phrased it, "the potentialities which different societies label as either masculine or feminine are really potentialities of some members of each sex, and not sex-linked at all."[15]

To describe a woman or girl as feminine seems innocuous enough, yet no matter how well intended, it reinforces the demand being made on her to conform to whatever standard of "femininity" is culturally accepted. On a science field trip for inner-city school children, the teacher invited a group of sixth-graders to look for specimens in a small stream. Within moments the boys had run down the bank and were knee-deep in muddy water. The girls hung back, self-conscious and apparently resentful at missing the fun. When one of the boys shouted up to them, "Why aren't there any girls down here?" a girl answered, "Because we're *girls,* that's why." "Because," she might as well have said, "we don't want anyone to think we're not feminine."[16] Betty Friedan cites a similar attitude among college women in the 1950s. As one senior explained, "A girl who got serious about anything she studied—like, wanting to go on and do research—would be peculiar, unfeminine."[17]

Margaret Mead believed masculine and feminine labels are even more destructive for a male who wants to depart from the cultural norm than they are for a female. Her point was that since men's activities are universally considered more prestigious than women's, the man or boy who is attuned by temperament to activities assigned to women loses more than the woman or girl who seeks fulfillment in fields considered proper only for males.[18] Yet our insistence on drawing up mental lists contrasting what is "masculine" with what is "feminine" diminishes not only individual women, but women as a class. It does so because male prestige is maintained by limiting female prestige—at the expense, ultimately, of the human wholeness of every individual.

Chapter 5

The Language of Religion

Nowhere are the semantic roadblocks to sexual equality more apparent—or significant—than in the language of the dominant organized religions. This is ironic but not surprising. Religious thinkers are forced to depend on symbols, particularly on metaphors and analogies, to describe and communicate to others what is by nature indescribable except in terms of human experience. The symbols are not intended to be taken literally but to point beyond themselves to a reality that can be only dimly perceived at best. "We must strain the poor resources of our language to express thoughts too great for words," Hilary of Poitiers wrote in the fourth century. "The error of others compels us to err in daring to embody in human terms truths which ought to be hidden in the silent veneration of the heart."[1]

Since the major Western religions all originated in patriarchal societies and continue to defend a patriarchal world view, the metaphors used to express their insights are by tradition and habit overwhelmingly male-oriented. As apologists of these religions have insisted for tens of centuries, the symbolization of a male God must not be taken to mean that God really *is* male. In fact, it must be understood that God has no sex at all. But inevitably, when words like *father* and *king* are used to evoke the image of a personal God, at some level of consciousness it is a male image that takes hold. And since the same symbols are used of male human beings—from whom, out of the need for analogy, the images of God have been drawn—female human beings become less God-like, less perfect, different, "the other." The most powerful symbols are often the simplest, those closest to experience—in the case of words, those we use daily, almost without thought. But these symbols can also lead most easily to distortion.

The linguist Mary Ritchie Key of the University of California at Irvine provides a pertinent example. In the Aztec language, which does not have masculine and feminine gender in its grammatical system, the third person singular pronoun *yejua* can refer to *he, she,* or *it.* Professor Key is convinced "that this is relevant to the concepts which the Aztecs devised for the explanation of their origins. They believed that the origin of the world and all human beings was *one single principle* with a dual nature. This supreme being had a male and female countenance—a dual god who conceived the universe, sustains it, and creates life."[2]

The god is called *Ometeotl,* from *ome* meaning "two" and *teotl* meaning "god." Sometimes the deity is described as having a partner or equal counterpart or is referred to by a term that means "the mother, the father, the old one." Yet despite the notion of plurality, the god is always spoken of in the singular grammatical form. There is a plural in Aztec if the ancients had wanted to use it, Key notes, but instead they referred to Ometeotl by the genderless third-person-singular pronoun *yejua.* Since our language has no personal pronoun equivalent to *yejua,* she points out, there is simply no way to translate the Aztec concept of a personal God into English.

"Nevertheless," Key says, "the eminent authorities who discuss Aztec religion all use the pronoun 'he' in the discussions. There is no more reason to use the male referent than to use 'she.' We can substitute the female referent just as correctly: 'She is Queen . . . and she rules.' " As for the concept of partner or equal, the translators use the words *wife* or consort. "Again, there is no word in English . . . to refer to this single dual being."

The authorities on Aztec religion are not the only translators who have allowed cultural or religious bias to affect their renderings of ancient texts. Phyllis Trible's analysis of the creation story in the second chapter of Genesis, discussed in Chapter 1, provides other examples: the translation of the Hebrew *'adham* as "man" rather than by a more inclusive term, and the choice of "help meet" or "helpmate" as the meaning of *'ezer.*[3] Neither rendering is a *mis*translation. When the Authorized (King James) Version of the Bible was completed in 1611, the Old English sense of *man* as "a person of either sex" was still recognized, though the word had already become ambiguous, and *'ezer* does not imply either grade or rank.[4] But no widely accepted translation has ever performed the urgently needed clarification of these Hebrew words by substituting a more accurate rendering of *man* to include both sexes, and not until 1970, when the New English Bible translated *'ezer* as "partner," has the connotation of "handmaiden" been corrected.

The female imagery used of God, which is clearly present in the Hebrew Scriptures along with male imagery, has often been ignored in English translations. When Moses, near the end of his life, speaks to the Israelites still wandering in the desert, he says (according to the King James Version of Deuteronomy 32:18), "Of the Rock that begat thee thou art unmindful, and hast forgotten God that formed thee." Two problems are involved.[5] The first is that the English word *beget* fails to convey here the full sense of the original Hebrew verb, which means either the begetting of a father or the bearing of a mother. Modern translations like the Revised Standard Version (1952), the Jerusalem Bible (1966), and the New English Bible (1970) repeat this limited interpretation, possibly because we have no equivalent in English to express the wider meaning conveyed in the Hebrew original. The second problem has been handled with varying degrees of fidelity. "Thou . . . hast forgotten God that formed thee" is not incorrect, but "formed" is an indefinite rendering of a Hebrew word that specifically describes the action of a woman in labor, and it is therefore never used of a man. The Revised Standard Version and the New English Bible come closer to the Hebrew in their wording "God who gave you birth" and "God who brought you to birth." Even so, the imagery in translation is not as strongly or exclusively female as it could be. The Jerusalem Bible is more than nonspecific. Its reading, "unmindful now of the God who fathered you," is at the same time patriarchal and erroneous.

The meanings of Greek texts have also sometimes been changed in biblical translations. For example, the King James reading of a familiar verse in the Gospel of John (16:21) says: "A woman when she is in travail hath sorrow, because her hour is come: but as soon as she is delivered of the child, she remembereth no more the anguish, for joy that a man is born into the world." Modern readers quite naturally attribute the woman's joy to the birth of a son. But the Greek word here translated "man" means "a human being,"[6] prompting the translators of the Revised Standard Version to say "for joy that a child is born into the world." Two more recent translations, however, the New English Bible and the Jerusalem Bible, again opt for "man."

In "Games Bible Translators Play," Ruth Hoppin, of the National Organization for Women Ecumenical Task Force on Women and Religion, notes several other instances in which masculine nouns and pronouns have been substituted for those of common gender. In the Gospel of John (1:12) and in the first Epistle of John (3:1 and 2), for example, the phrase "sons of God" occurs in the King James Version, a reading changed to "children of God" in most contemporary translations.[7] In view of the enormous weight given by Christians to every word of the New Testament, particularly the Gospels, the use of "sons" is not easily explained.

While Western religions have traditionally portrayed the spiritual nature of human beings and their relation to God in male terms, sexuality is portrayed as female, the embodiment of sin, forever distracting men from godliness: "sons of God" but "daughters of Eve." Catalysts in a cosmic struggle between evil and good, women are defined as extremes of the sexuality men experience—whore or virgin, agent of Satan or mother of God.

When he was dean of the Harvard Divinity School, Krister Stendahl commented on the serious nature of male-centered religious imagery and linked the way Christians speak about God with the way they tend to think about God. "All good theologians," he said, with more tolerance, perhaps, than accuracy, "have always been in tune with that story about the person who came back from heaven and told what God looked like, saying: She is black." Stendahl went on:

> The masculinity of God, and of God-language is a cultural and linguistic accident, and I think one should also argue that the masculinity of the Christ is of the same order. To be sure, Jesus Christ was a male, but that may be no more significant to his being than the fact that presumably his eyes were brown. Incarnation is a great thing. But it strikes me as odd to argue that when the Word became flesh, it was to reenforce male superiority.
>
> Much so-called liberal theology has a special problem here, for it has tended to increase the anthropomorphism of Christian language. In moving away from the deeper

> aspects of trinitarian speculation, it centered more and more on the idea of God as the Father and made the imagery of Fatherhood the overarching metaphor for God. One started with the idea of "Father" and blew it up into divine proportions. The old process was reversed: Instead of saying that the One who created the world and nurtured the galaxies could even be called "Father" by the mystery of faith, anthropomorphism won out and the Father image became supreme. A metaphor of faith, with a specific and limited intention, hardened into a concept that was not checked by genuine transcendence, and it became trivialized. The time has come to liberate our thoughts of God from such sexism; and a richer trinitarian speculation with the Spirit (which happens to be female in Hebrew) may be one way toward that goal. It is obvious that those who say "God" and mean it cannot accept a male God without falling into idolatry.
>
> . . . Such attempts at rethinking and re-experiencing call for a critique and renewal of the traditional language of theology and liturgy and everyday life. For that reason I take the matter of pronouns seriously. To many, such concerns seem trivial or ridiculous. They are not. Language is powerful. Generic "man" is a real obstacle to the digested understanding and feeling of "male and female created he them."[8]

About a year before Dean Stendahl made these remarks, two Harvard Divinity School students, Linda Barufoldi and Emily Culpepper, who were enrolled in a course taught by Harvey G. Cox, had called for "concerted efforts in the lectures and discussions of this course no longer to use sexist language." As reported in the *Harvard Crimson,* "The proposal specifically called for a ban on the use of 'Man,' 'Men' and masculine pronouns 'to refer to all people.' It also urged that masculine names and pronouns not be used with reference to God." The class voted overwhelmingly to adopt the proposal,[9] which Professor Cox characterized as responding to "the basic theological question of whether God is more adequately thought of in personal or suprapersonal terms."[10]

The incident received wide coverage, including an article in *Newsweek,* which labeled it "yet another tilt at the windmill" and called the students "distaff theologians."[11] This tongue-in-cheek attention did not occur, however, until seventeen members of the university's Department of Linguistics, including the department's distinguished chair, Calvert Watkins, had written a letter to the *Crimson* on the subject of the students' action. The proposal "to recast part of the grammar of the English language reflects a concern which we as linguists would like to try to alleviate," the letter began, and it then explained the properties of what linguists call "marked and unmarked" pairs.

> Many of the grammatical and lexical oppositions in language are not between equal members of a pair but between two entities one of which is more "marked" than the other (to use the technical term). . . .
>
> For people and pronouns in English the masculine is the unmarked and hence is used as a neutral or unspecified term. This reflects the ancient pattern of the Indo-European languages. . . . The fact that the masculine is the unmarked gender in English (or that the feminine is unmarked in the language of the Tunica Indians) is simply a feature of grammar. It is unlikely to be an impediment to any change in the patterns of the sexual division of labor toward which our society may wish to evolve. There is really no cause for anxiety or pronoun-envy on the part of those seeking such changes.[12]

Professor Watkins was apparently ignoring his own insights on the interaction of language and culture already quoted in Chapter 4. It was this very interaction, however, that James L.

Armagost of the Department of Linguistics at the University of Washington called attention to in a letter commenting on his fellow linguists' explanation of marked and unmarked terms: "A reasonably inquisitive person might wonder why the masculine is unmarked. The question deserves a better answer than: 'What a coincidence that the masculine is unmarked in the language of a people convinced that men are superior to women.' "[13] Randall Blake Michael, a member of Professor Cox's class, also sensed the deep currents of pain his fellow students were expressing. The *Newsweek* account "does not seem to recognize that language, including pronouns, is capable of participating in the reality to which human beings must react and respond," he wrote. "Our society's oppressive nature is all too obvious and all too real to these female human beings; and their expressions of pain should not be dismissed as a party game."[14]

How tendentious the whole issue of God's "sex" becomes was demonstrated by the Episcopal bishop of California, the Right Reverend C. Kilmer Myers, in a statement opposing the ordination of women to the priesthood. "A priest is a 'God-symbol' whether he likes it or not," Myers wrote. "In the imagery of both the Old and New Testaments God is represented in masculine imagery. The father begets the Son. This is essential to the *givingness* of the Christian Faith, and to tamper with this imagery is to change that Faith to something else." But "this does not mean God is a male," the bishop continued, for "biblical language is the language of analogy. It is imperfect, even as all human imagery of God must be imperfect. Nevertheless, it has meaning. The male image about God pertains to the divine initiative in creation. Initiative is, in itself, a male rather than a female attribute. . . . The generative function is plainly a masculine kind of imagery, making priesthood a masculine conception."[15]

Conception? The word is a curious one to use in this context, bringing to mind as it does the union of ovum and sperm. And curious, too, is the notion that *givingness* is somehow more of a male than a female attribute, especially in the context of "generative function." The bishop's theology here, as well as his biology, appears to be based on the linguistic assignment to males of exclusive credit for procreation. From the begettings of scripture to the latest seminal idea for saving the world, the English language tells us that males alone are responsible for new life. According to this biology, the male inseminates whereas the female merely incubates. It is a scientific inaccuracy still reflected in the very different meanings assigned to the verbs "to father" and "to mother"—and it remains a potent factor in traditional theological formulations of God's nature.

Religious educators maintain that to use literal images in teaching children about religious faith does not limit a child's ability to reach a more mature understanding, provided the metaphorical concepts are such that adult faith can be built on them. Certainly from all the evidence available, a child, in modern times at least, would have to be a religious prodigy not to visualize some kind of human male figure out of all the masculine pronouns and the imagery of *father, lord, king* used to describe the deity. That many do is illustrated in a small book called *Children's Letters to God.* A special poignancy leaps from one page: "Dear God," wrote a little girl named Sylvia. "Are boys better than girls. I know you are one but try to be fair."[16]

The test of a metaphor, said Robert H. Thouless, a British psychiatrist and reader in educational theology at Cambridge University, is not whether it is true or false, but whether it is adequate. "The test of adequacy," he wrote, "is whether it leads to understanding of and appropriate behaviour with respect to the thing referred to."[17] When women challenge the masculine linguistic symbols for God, what they are asking, among other things, is whether these metaphors do not encourage a double standard for evaluating human beings in addition to reinforcing an idolatrous concept of the deity.

In an effort to avoid the overmasculinized symbolization of modern Christianity it has become popular to speak of the "masculine" and "feminine" attributes of God. But this is a case of out of the frying pan into the fire, for as already noted, no words are more slippery or more given to stereotyping than these. Some religious thinkers shy away from such an obvious cultural trap—"We have to stop either masculinizing or feminizing God and go for something fundamentally different"[18] sums up their position—but from the Vatican to the smallest village congregation other religious leaders seem all too eager to divide everything in life into sex-differentiated categories as a way of counteracting past prejudices, and they end up deepening the dilemma. For unless the categorizers have reached a level of understanding that frees them from at least the grossest cultural preconceptions in applying to God the words *feminine* and *masculine,* they merely add the weight of religious sanction to the polarization that stifles genuine individual distinctions.

"I would suggest the following parallel list as descriptive of the difference between the masculine and feminine sides of life," a minister wrote in his weekly newsletter, and he appended the following sets of words:

rational, ordered	spontaneous, free
form, plan	matter, context, content
authority	supportiveness
penetrating, aggressive	receptive, submissive
linear, pointed	voluminous, containing
government	community
direction	area, space

"Few would have trouble picking the left side as the masculine side and the right as the feminine side," the minister observed. "It is not merely a matter of cultural upbringing, since all of life, even physical objects, can be shown to have its masculine and feminine sides. Where cultural bias comes in is in the assignment of these various characteristics to the male or female."[19]

Yet that is precisely what the writer has done in imposing a "masculine-feminine" division on all of life, even physical objects. For what do "masculine" and "feminine" (as distinct from "male" and "female") mean except that they describe characteristics a given culture assigns to or associates with males or females? Can any culture that makes such assignments—and all do—be without bias from the viewpoint of another culture whose parallel lists of "masculine" and "feminine" characteristics are quite different? It is hard to see what can be gained, pedagogically or theologically, by still another list of such contrasts. Apart from its transparent sexual analogies, the characteristics it assigns to "the masculine and feminine sides of life" do, however, reinforce a sex-role division consistent with Judeo-Christian cultural traditions.

In *Thinking About Women* Mary Ellmann tackles the problem of such analogies from a different perspective. She is speaking of the space program and what it has to say about strength and weakness:

> The shape of the rocket no doubt misleads many observers, along the cement paths of Freudian correspondences, to a masculine conception of the program. But its human role is not energetic or forceful. . . . Like a woman being carted to a delivery room, the astronaut must sit (or lie) still, and go where he is sent. Even the nerve, the genuine courage it takes simply not to run away, is much the same in both situations—to say nothing of the shared sense of having gone too far to be able to change one's mind.
>
> It is, then, a time in which sexual differences are more visual than actual. We *see* a man doing what we would ordinarily think of as feminine, sitting still, and manage to think of it as masculine because a man is doing it. . . . Perhaps as long as sexual interest in any sense is strong, we will continue to comprehend all phenomena, however shifting, in terms of our original and simple sexual differences; and to classify almost all experiences by means of sexual analogy.

> The persistence of the habit is even, conceivably, admirable. It might be taken as proof of the fertility of the human mind that, given so little sexual evidence, it should contrive so large a body of dependent sexual opinion.[20]

Mortmain, a word that literally means "dead hand," came into being as a legal term referring to the perpetual ownership of lands by ecclesiastical or other authorities. "There was a time when the thought of Christendom was in mortmain no less than its land," J. B. Mayor wrote in 1876,[21] and a hundred years later women find themselves still oppressed by the dead hand of sexist theology. Their new self-awareness opens perspectives that in the past have been obscured by "a male-centered cultural and religious heritage which continues to assume that man sets the standards and is the norm for being human."[22]

The words just quoted are from the report of a conference of theologians, all of whom were women. The dual role of language in expressing experience and conditioning it, and the historical fact that males have been the namers and definers and, if not the sole originators, at least the chief interpreters of religious metaphors, were recurring conference themes. In the course of exploring new theological models, one of the concepts that evolved was the need for a greater emphasis on verbs rather than on nouns, the need to speak, for example, of "ruling" rather than of "king." Positions of power have traditionally been held by men, and so the noun forms used to describe images of power have for the most part been masculine. Women, however, have exerted power in other areas of life, the conference report noted. "Since the verb is a more dynamic form, it is more open to additional meaning that women's experience may bring to it." The greater use of verbs would also avoid "attempts to place both masculine and feminine qualities in God," a step that tends "to eternalize what we now understand as social and historical cultural conditioning."[23]

The radical theologian Mary Daly is also interested in the

liberating power of verb forms—of "God" as "Being," for example—and in the power of naming.

> The myth of the Fall . . . amounts to a cosmic false naming. It misnames the mystery of evil, casting it into the distorted mold of the myth of feminine evil. In this way images and conceptualizations about evil are thrown out of focus and its deepest dimensions are not really confronted. . . .
>
> Out of the surfacing woman-consciousness is coming the realization that the basic counteraction to patriarchy's false naming of evil has to come primarily from women. By dislodging ourselves from the role of "the Other" . . . women are dislodging the mystery of evil from this false context and thus clearing the way for seeing and naming it more adequately.[24]

When Daly speaks of naming she refers to bringing into being "a new meaning context . . . as we re-create our lives in a new experiential context." She says, "to exist humanly is to name the self, the world, and God."[25]

> The "method" of the evolving spiritual consciousness of women is nothing less than a reclaiming of the right to name.
>
> It would be a mistake to imagine that the new speech of women can be equated simply with women speaking men's words. What is happening is that women are *hearing* each other and ourselves for the first time, and out of this supportive hearing emerge *new words.* Words that, materially speaking, are identical with the old become new in a semantic context that emerges from qualitatively new experience. Thus the word "sisterhood," wrenched from its patriarchal context, no longer means a subordinate semi-brotherhood but an authentic bonding of women.[26]

To Mary Daly, the essential thing is "to hear our *own* words, always giving prior attention to our *own* experience, never letting prefabricated theory have authority over us."[27]

Woman as temptress, the eternal Eve, the gateway to hell, and woman as virgin, pure, undefiled keeper of hearth and home are polarized images in Western religious thought—impossible extremes of evil and good that leave no place for a real person. But as women free themselves to reflect on their own experiences and human longings, they are creating new images and symbols that will bring into being not a "feminine" or even a feminist theology, but new, more inclusive ways of describing the indescribable.

Chapter 6

THE GREAT MALE PLOT

Critics of the women's movement seem bewitched by the idea that feminists attribute the linguistic oppression of women to an organized conspiracy. According to one such thinker, feminists believe that "men have traditionally used language to subjugate women," and if he had only stopped there he would have left little room for argument. But he went on: "As they see it, William James' bitch-goddess Success and the National Weather Service's Hurricane Agnes are products of the same criminal mind, designed to foster the illusion of woman as Eve, forever volatile and treacherous."[1]

Now, the suggestion of a criminal mind at work is an intriguing thought. Over the centuries women have fared very badly indeed in the English language. They lost their job titles and acquired substitutes applicable to women only. They acquired social titles advertising their married or unmarried state and on marriage lost their own last names. Their contribution to procreation was linguistically obscured if not actually denied. Their mythic foremothers were given derivative titles like *goddess* and *heroine* and, through words like *venereal* and *aphrodisiac,* some were associated with sexuality but none with triumphs of the mind or spirit. Women really lost ground when the maleness of *man* overpowered its humanness. Along the way even God acquired a male identity, and the legal profession tended to lose sight of women's very existence. In 1894, for example, a woman was denied entry to the Virginia bar when the Supreme Court of the United States ruled it was reasonable for a lower court to determine that a "woman" was not a "person."[2]

Of course, all these semantic setbacks may have happened in the natural course of events, but the suggestion of a criminal mind at work—a conspiracy of male linguists burning the midnight oil to come up with new ways of subverting the language to their own ends—ignites the imagination. The organization must be quite large. How long has it been going on, and where do the brothers meet?

Imagine picking up the morning paper and reading:

> JOHANNESBURG, South Africa, August 1—The one hundred and twenty-fifth plenary session of Men Against Linguistic Equality (MALE) opened here today on a note of urgency as the largest number of participants in the society's history renewed their vows "to keep the English language working for us."
>
> Although press coverage of the event was barred, a source who did not wish to be identified stated that the society is facing its greatest challenge since its founding twelve hundred and fifty years ago. He said it would be "unwise" for him to elaborate.
>
> MALE is the English-speaking branch of an international secret brotherhood known to have existed since the third millennium B.C. Founded in Sumeria to combat the influence of the world's first poet, Enheduanna, who through her writing established the cultic primacy of the

female deity Inanna, the organization is still dedicated to the belief, according to one member, "that women should be seen and not heard."

The parent organization is said to have functioned without interruption since its inception and to include branches representing every major language in the world. MALE, the organization's largest branch, has chapters in all English-speaking countries and in most other major capitals.

MALE claims to represent 360 million people whose native language is English and at least an additional 45 million to whom English is a second tongue. In a statement issued yesterday from the Washington headquarters of the National Organization for Women, this claim was disputed as "ridiculous and childish" on the grounds that over half of all English-speaking people are female and "vigorously oppose their subjugation through language." MALE is reliably reported to maintain, however, that "women have no minds of their own and are therefore numbered only in body counts."

Although the existence of MALE has been recognized since its infiltration in 1876 by a group calling itself the John Stuart Mill Brigade, little is known of the organization's structure, history, or the influences on English for which it claims credit.

The 1966 plenary session of MALE, held at the Bohemian Grove, near Monte Rio, California, was the first meeting to receive publicity, a consequence, it is believed, of internal dissent over how to defuse the feminist countermovement which works openly in political, educational, and corporate spheres to expose MALE's previously concealed influence on the language.

Stung by the growing acceptance of the social title Ms. and of changes in political and occupational nomenclature, as well as by "nonsexist guidelines" issued by several major

American publishing houses, a number of men believed to hold important leadership positions in MALE have adopted the tactic of open counterattack through ridicule.

The majority of members, however, are said to support the organization's traditional strategy of working behind the scenes to influence grammarians, usage experts, teachers, and others who mold the thinking of children. This so-called "Schoolmasters" approach relies on the early inculcation of language habits, presumably in the belief that once indoctrinated, future leaders in the arts, sciences, education, government, and industry will continue to employ language habits that work to exclude or downgrade women through subsuming and belittling terminology.

MALE's militant faction argues that beginning with the universal education of females in the 19th century, the indirect, "Schoolmasters" approach ceased to be effective. The Johannesburg sessions are expected to revolve around this issue.

The organization's unalterable rule that all meetings be held "in the buff" has successfully kept women from gaining admission to any session of the brotherhood. Until now rigorous investigation of every member's published works has also been effective in barring men suspected of sympathizing with women over what has recently become known as "sexist language." Scholarly research and the ground swell of protest on the part of women and their male supporters, however, has led to renewed fears that the current session may be breached by defectors from within MALE's ranks. Security is therefore assumed to be at an all-time high.

The meetings will continue through August 5.

Far-fetched as an organization dedicated to opposing linguistic equality may sound, some of the rebuttals male writers have come up with since women began crying foul—and the amount of space self-respecting publications have allotted to them—make an imaginary group like MALE tantalizingly plausible.

Columnist William F. Buckley, Jr., for example, without explaining his use of the word "us," moaned in 1972, "Somebody has got to rescue us from the women's liberation movement." He was staging a skirmish against the Scott, Foresman "Guidelines for Improving the Image of Women in Textbooks," the first nonsexist guidelines for writers and editors issued by a major textbook publisher. But Buckley's usual wit was blunted. Though his efforts ranged from a joke about women drivers to a consideration of whether Galileo was better looking than Marie Curie, he failed to score. For example, the guidelines, having made the point that "occupational terms often ignore the existence of women workers," suggest the use of "terms that reflect the actual composition of a group." As alternatives to "businessmen; congressmen; mailmen; repairmen; etc. when women are part of these groups," they offer "businessmen and women, business people; members of Congress, congressmen and women; mail carriers; someone to repair the . . ."[3]

Buckley took exception to the lot, and ignoring the guidelines' carefully stated context, not to mention people like the publisher Katharine Graham, Representative Shirley Chisholm, and Josephine the Plumber, commented:

> "Businessmen" is out: "business people" is in. Presumably the singular is a "business person." What do you want to be when you grow up, Johnny? A business person. What do you do with "repairmen"? Not even Scott Foresman dared come up with "repairperson," so they offer: "someone to repair the . . ." which can be spotted as a syntactical cop-out in sexist and nonsexist societies.[4]

Might not the so-called cop-out better be called a useful resolution of a syntactical cut-out? Another Buckley complaint was even less cogent:

> They are so carried away, over at Scott Foresman, that they appear to have lost all sense of inflection. For instance, the sexist "The ancient Egyptians allowed women considerable control over property" has got to be changed to "Women in ancient Egypt had considerable control over property"—which is, very simply, a totally different statement from the first.[5]

Different and neat. Carried away by his own fervor, Buckley lost sight of what the first statement assumes—which is, very simply, that all ancient Egyptians were males.

Subsequently, Buckley's colleague and fellow columnist George F. Will took a more serious approach to another publisher's similar guidelines. He wrote:

> A European critic once noted that "what American women suffer from is too much poor-quality attention." Certainly intelligent women must cringe at the kind of attention lavished on women in a depressing document titled "Guidelines for Equal Treatment of the Sexes in McGraw-Hill Book Company Publications."[6]

George Will does not try for humor. He is, as he says, depressed. But neither does he try to explain his antipathy or why, for example, he calls the guidelines "embarrassing," "banal," and "pathetic" rather than "welcome," "refreshing," and "long-overdue." Or perhaps the explanation is lost among his accusations of "huffing and puffing," "tinkering," "truculence," and "niggling." Could a possible clue to the author's tone lie in the following?

> Although I am of the male persuasion, even I understand that the unequal status of women is an irrational waste of talent in most societies. But it will not be rectified by people who waste time blaming and banning the kind of language that the McGraw-Hill guideline writers object to. . . ."[7]

If one overlooks the temptation to ask in which societies Will thinks the unequal status of women is *not* an irrational waste of talent, one is left with the strange phrase, "Although I am of the male persuasion . . ." Since one meaning of *persuasion* is "a faction; sect; party" and since it is supererogation for a male writer named George (unlike a female writer named George) to announce his sex, could the explanation be . . . ? Just spell "male" in capital letters and the message is clear: one of the brothers doing his zealous best for the Brotherhood!

Still another form of rebuttal appeals to writers who like to fool around with words the way first-graders do. The genre would be less tedious if only, once started, its devotees knew how to stop; but like six-year-olds, they tend to reach dizzying heights of self-titillation, driving themselves on to one more and yet one more bit of nonsense. *Time* magazine essayist Stefan Kanfer's contribution read in part: "Shedonism, girlcotting and countess-downs were to be anticipated in the liberated '70s. As for the enemy, he could expect to be confronted by female belligerents inviting him to put up his duchesses. He would find, in short, that his gander was cooked. All flagrantly gendered words would be swiftly unsexed. The ottoman would become the otto-it, the highboy would metamorphose into the high-thing, and ladyfingers would be served under the somewhat less appealing name of personfingers."[8]

New York Times humorist Russell Baker set a new record for endurance. After some fifteen column-inches devoted to replacing *man* with *person,* he ended: "Like—person—you know! Where's your personners, person? You've been personipulating me! I must get back to serious thinking about the President's persondate, the persontle of greatness, penpersonship, oneupspersonship, the decline of the praying persontis, Persondrake the Magician and whether the Presidency is still attainable by Governor . . . Rockefolk."[9]

While executive editor of the American Heritage Publishing Company's Dictionary Division, Alma Graham got so many letters written in this vein that she decided to marshal some deadpan etymological evidence to deal with a few of the favorites. For example, the *man* in *manager, management, manuscript, manners, manipulate, manufacture,* and *manifest* comes from the Latin *manus,* "hand." The *man* in *mandate* is from the Latin *mandare,* "to command" and that in *mantle* from the Latin *mantellum,* "cloak." The Proto-Algonquian *menahanwi,* meaning island, gave us *Manhattan; mañana* is from the Latin *mane,* "in the morning"; and *mania* comes from the Greek word meaning madness. The *man* in *human* is as much female as male since the word goes back to the Latin *humanus,* which in turn goes back to the Indo-European root meaning earthling, the same root that gave rise to the Latin *homo* and the Old English *mann.*[10]

Woman, then, is not derived from a word that originally meant a male, as purveyors of *woperson, wobody,* or *wo* would have us believe. Contrary to at least one scholarly opinion,[11] its origin was not "wife" (in the modern sense) plus "man"; it was "female" plus "human being." Nor is *female* a derivative of *male.* A Middle English variant of the Old French *femelle,* from the Latin diminutive of *femina,* meaning "woman," *female* has no etymological connection with *male* at all; its present spelling and pronunciation evolved only because people mistakenly assumed it did.

Among the many influences that have shaped our language the part played by individuals is relatively small. But almost from its beginnings, about fifteen hundred years ago, English has been molded and modified, nudged toward change here and held intact there by people who have made the language their special province. Not coincidentally, these people were rarely female before the last few decades. The observation by the great Danish linguist Otto Jespersen in the 1920s that "the science of language has very few votaries among women"[12] is no longer true. But it applied for more than four thousand years after Enheduanna, the Sumerian poet.[13]

To suggest that the majority of language votaries have been woman-haters would be incorrect. On the contrary, most have been exceptionally civilized gentlemen who had a high regard for specific women—at least, one likes to think, for those who bore them and for others whom they loved, married, or fathered. But it is largely in terms of these relationships to *themselves* that they have perceived females when writing about the language that presumably belongs to both sexes. For example, Lincoln Barnett, an eloquent historian of English, reminds his readers that the original Old English vocabulary consisted of about thirty thousand words, of which only some 15 percent survive today. "Yet the survivors make up the basic building blocks of our language," he writes, ". . . describing the quintessential things of life and human existence: *man, wife, child. . . .*"[14]

The early English of which Barnett was speaking had a powerful champion in Alfred the Great, the Anglo-Saxon king who in the ninth century encouraged the widespread literary use of English, as opposed to Latin, and who is responsible for the high level of prose recorded in his native tongue. In that tongue, as already mentioned, *man* meant a human being of either sex, and *wif* and *wer* were the words for an adult female and male respectively. The parallel usage was somewhat analogous to the relative status of women and men in the society. Women had personal and property rights equal to those of men, and they worked at a wide variety of trades.

By the end of the fifteenth century, the point marking the transition from Middle English to Modern English, women's options had been greatly reduced and their rights curtailed under English common law.[15] Their diminished status relative to men was symbolized in the growing exclusion of women from the very word *men. Wer* had by now dropped out of the language, though it survived in a few combinations like *werewolf* and the legal term *wergild,* which was a payment to a dead man's family by the person responsible for his death. *Man* and *men* were used increasingly for males only, leaving no unequivocal monosyllable that included members of both sexes.

It also happened that English at this time was being enriched by a great influx of words from the classical languages and from French and Italian. Many foreign terms were deliberately introduced by translators and scholars like Sir Thomas Elyot, author of the first Latin-English dictionary, who set out, as he wrote in 1531, to "augment our English tongue, whereby men should express more abundantly the thing that they conceived in their hearts (wherefore language was ordained) having words apt for the purpose."[16] Unfortunately, it does not seem to have occurred to Elyot or any other scholar that the deficit in English caused by the growing ambiguity of *man* might be remedied by importing a new word either for a human being or a human male.

The renaissance of learning in England at the beginning of the sixteenth century heralded not only the extraordinary flowering of English literature over the next hundred years but the extension of education from the nobility to commoners. This development was aided by the invention of movable type, a contribution of the previous century, and the subsequent printing of English translations of the Bible. William Tyndale's translation of the New Testament, one of the actions for which the author was condemned and burned at the stake in 1536, accomplished his aim of bringing the scriptures within reach of "the boy that draweth the plow," though it left the plowboy's sister no better off than she had been.

Interest in the education of girls continued to be nonexistent except among the elite whose daughters were taught reading and writing—primarily to increase their value as attractive and useful companions to their husbands and fathers. Women might even learn foreign and classical languages, but if they displayed an aptitude for scholarship, it was likely to be discouraged. Margaret More (later Margaret Roper) was a case in point. She was a brilliant student of Greek and Latin and the daughter of Sir Thomas More, one of the most just and reasoning men of his time. According to legend, Margaret was engaged in compiling a Latin concordance to the Bible when one day her father found her in tears over her work. As the British writer Margaret Lawrence describes the scene:

> He took the manuscript gently from her, and explained to her that such was not a woman's work. . . . He was kind, and said he was proud of her desire to do the task, but to allow her to do it would be a mistake. It would consume her, he explained, and leave no residue either of emotion, or thought, and that would be very sad for her happiness as a woman. Women, he taught her, must save all their energies for the race. With his fine clear perception of things he turned her imagination softly away from scholarship, and directed it upon one whom he called "yon tall stripling," and Margaret, who adored her father, believed him to be right, and obeyed him.[17]

This was the gentle way a loving father precluded the possibility of even a scholarly woman's full participation in the science and art of language. At the other extreme were the experiences of anonymous women whose potential genius in language fell victim not only to their enforced illiteracy but to male expectations. Virginia Woolf provided a striking picture of such an anonymous woman. Shakespeare had a sister Judith, Woolf imagines, who was extraordinarily gifted and "as adventurous, as imaginative, as agog to see the world" as her brother. While he went to school to learn the elements of grammar and logic, she mended stockings and minded the stew. Secretly she studied her brother's schoolbooks and "perhaps she scribbled some pages up in an apple loft on the sly." But when she ran away to London and asked for a job at the theater where her brother had once held horses at the stage door, she was scorned and ridiculed. She could get no training, nor even a job to pay for a meal or a place to sleep. Finally, after the theater manager had taken pity on her, "she found herself with child by that gentleman and so—who shall measure the heat and violence of the poet's heart when caught and tangled in a woman's body?—killed herself one winter's night and lies buried at some crossroads where the omnibuses now stop outside the Elephant and Castle."[18]

Girls with no special literary drive or imagination must have been as numerous as Shakespeare's schoolboy "creeping like a snail unwillingly to school." But motivated girls lacked even a basic tool to use in teaching themselves until dictionaries were available. The first English dictionaries, which appeared early in the seventeenth century, were modeled on bilingual dictionaries and were concerned, according to a modern high school textbook on language, "with helping the literate man to read literature written in a foreign language, or to help a literate man understand the meanings of foreign words that had been borrowed by his language."[19] As books of foreign words and "hard words" proliferated, the compilers plagiarized from one another in an effort to increase their word lists, and some accused others of including even "trivial words." Among the chief beneficiaries of this practice were women who with little or no schooling now managed to become literate anyway.

The early English dictionaries contain evidence of the intention to exploit this new female market. According to the etymologist Ernest Weekley, their publishers consistently emphasized that they catered to "the class intermediate between the educated gentleman and the illiterate peasant, a class defined on one title page as consisting of 'Young Scholars, Tradesmen, Artificers, and the female Sex,' on another as 'Ladies who have a turn for Reading and Gentlemen of no learned Profession.' "

Still another dictionary, Weekley notes, described itself as "chiefly intended for the more-knowing Women and less-knowing Men."[20]

Dictionary making came into its own in the eighteenth century with Samuel Johnson's monumental work, which was intended for everyone, not just for intermediate classes like the female sex. At about the same time, however, language votaries were advocating a new notion that was to gain a stranglehold on the minds of educated speakers of English on both sides of the Atlantic. This notion, in the words of Thomas Pyles, a modern historian of English, was "that the language is of divine origin and hence was perfect in its beginnings but is constantly in danger of corruption and decay unless it is diligently kept in line by wise men who are able to get themselves accepted as authorities, for instance, men who write dictionaries and grammars."[21] (It was the perfect climate to bring MALE's Schoolmasters faction into flower.)

Among the chief proponents of the idea that language must be diligently guarded was Jonathan Swift, who in 1712 proposed that the government establish an academy of scholars for the purpose of "correcting, improving and ascertaining the English tongue." Seventy-eight years later in the United States John Adams urged Congress to establish a similar academy on the grounds that "all the states of the Union are so democratized that eloquence will become the instrument for recommending men to their fellow citizens and the principal means of advancement through the various ranks and offices of society."[22]

Though the proposed academies never materialized, learned men who were able to get themselves accepted as authorities succeeded in establishing the "proper" use of English for the next several centuries. It was one of the first of these, the English grammarian George Campbell, who inadvertently confirmed the demise of the generic meaning of *man.* Writing in the 1770s, he noted the illogic of calling a certain type of sailing vessel a "merchantman" or a "man of war" when sailors commonly refer to their ships as "she."[23] None of the early grammarians seems to have commented on the illogic of referring to an indefinite person as "he," however, and their followers established a rule not only sanctioning but requiring this illogical usage—a "rule" that had already been broken by Sir Thomas More, Shakespeare, Fielding, Goldsmith, and Thackeray, among others.

No doubt a George Campbell Chapter of MALE still survives, but a name even more revered by the brethren must surely be that of the late H. W. Fowler, author of *A Dictionary of Modern English Usage.* Fowler was a stickler for precision—"words used must . . . actually yield on scrutiny the desired sense," he once wrote[24]—but he had a number of blind spots, especially on the subject of the linguistic equality of the sexes and the precise meaning of such off-again-on-again words as *man* and *he.*

"*As anybody can see for themselves*" is a phrase that "sets the literary man's teeth on edge," Fowler said. He was approving the "convention that where the matter of sex is not conspicuous or important *he* & *his* shall be allowed to represent a person instead of a man, or," he added for clarification, "a man (homo) instead of a man (vir)."[25] But as anybody can see for themselves, sex is always important when the accomplishments of one sex are being co-opted by the other. Even as Fowler explained the pronoun convention, he illustrated its perversity by associating it with "the literary man." As this is the same Fowler who protested that the literary woman should be content to be called an "authoress" or "poetess"—designations most likely to set her teeth on edge—one may well ask who this "literary man" is. Is "he" also "a person instead of a man"? Or, as Fowler explained when the apparently unexpected ambiguity encroached on his precision, "a man (homo) instead of a man (vir)"? Nowhere else in *Modern English Usage* does he distinguish between the two meanings or discuss the need to do so.

Otto Jespersen, Fowler's contemporary, called him an "instinctive grammatical moralizer." The two men did not agree on their approach to the study of language, the former being a "grammatical historian," the latter a "prescriptive grammarian." According to Jespersen, descriptive rather than prescriptive grammar is of greater value, for "instead of acting as a guide to what should be said or written, [it] aims at finding out what is actually said or written by those who use the language." Fowler's intention, on the other hand, was "to tell the people not what they do and how they came to do it, but what they ought to do for the future."[26] (Obviously, Jespersen's credentials would not have passed muster for membership in MALE; Fowler's would have been flawless.)

The arguments that exploded in 1961 over the publication of Webster's Third New International Dictionary were drawn along much the same lines. American authorities on the proper use of English were—practically to a man—wrathful. In the controversy over this major reference work, critics claimed that Webster's had abdicated its "authority" by failing to label usage "good" or "bad." Webster's editors countered that their authority lay in describing how words were currently being used, not in prescribing how they should be used.

What many of those who disparaged this dictionary ignored was that, despite the efforts of schoolmasters, the English language as spoken in America had changed considerably in the three decades since the publication of the second unabridged Webster's. As though to emphasize this oversight, *Life* magazine reached back to revive some ancient clichés when it editorialized, "Webster's, joining in the say-as-you-go school of permissive English, has now all but abandoned any attempt to distinguish between good and bad usage—between the King's English, say, and the fishwife's."[27] Was it merely a lapse of memory regarding the sex of Elizabeth II that caused *Life* to ignore the information, contained in both the second and third editions of Webster's, that "the Queen's English" is used when the reigning British monarch is a woman? Perhaps so, but in dredging up the fishwife to represent "bad usage," the editorial illustrates another archaic bias that persists in spite of hundreds of thousands of amiable, well-spoken women all over the English-speaking world who make their living selling fish.

Fears for the future of English provoked by the new dictionary were summed up by Garry Wills, who wrote in the *National Review* that language "has been shaped by man's mind, and like all other things with their source in man, it tends constantly to go shapeless." Condemning Webster's Third as "for-by-and-of The People," he went on to predict that "our language will be saved, if it is not too late, by harder men, men willing to discipline themselves in the use of language, men not willing to let others smash what has been formed with such effort. Such men do not think communication is advanced by the surrender of definition"—and so on and on.[28]

(Although the evidence is circumstantial only, MALE-watchers speculate that the first breaks in MALE's unilateral strategy date from this period, having been triggered by alarm over Webster's "permissive" approach and the effective defense of this approach in reviews written by two women, Millicent Taylor in the *Christian Science Monitor* and Ethel Strainchamps in the *Saint Louis Post-Dispatch.*[29])

Even the severest critics of Webster's Third admire the vitality of English, and whether it appears to go shapeless or to assume new shapes depends on one's point of view. The fact is, of course, that like any other living language, it changes constantly. Over the decades and centuries words shed some of their meanings and extend others: a *girl* was once a young person of either sex, for example; a *knave* was a boy, not a scoundrel; and a *gossip* meant a sponsor in baptism. Old words add new meanings: a *camper* can now have four wheels instead of two legs, and *camping,* far from roughing it, can mean behaving "effeminately." Some words, like *wer,* drop out of use entirely, and at least one, *man,* narrowed its meaning by half and subsumed the other half in an equivocal generalization that sometimes does and sometimes does not include everybody. "Me Tarzan, you Jane" became, you might say, "Me species, you subspecies."

What all this comes down to is that the male bias of English did not have to be fostered by a conspiracy. It came about through the working of a familiar principle: power tends to corrupt. English is male-oriented because it evolved through centuries of patriarchy to meet the needs of patriarchy. Those in power tend to try to stay there, and those out of power, to make the best of what they are allotted. But because women's image of themselves is changing, language is changing in response. Generations of women, taught to value the accomplishments of their husbands (or fathers or brothers or sons) more highly than their own, made an emotional investment in being identified through males. However, once enough wives, daughters, sisters, and mothers began to say, "But I have my own identity," new wheels were set in motion, new life-styles began to appear, and new linguistic symbols emerged to describe them. All of which can be seen in the recent history of women's social titles.

The abbreviation *Ms.* has been around as a title of courtesy since at least the 1940s, but it was largely unused until two things happened: the growth of direct-mail selling made the abbreviation an effective time- and money-saver, and a significant number of women began to object to being labeled according to their (presumed) marital status.

The 1972 American Heritage School Dictionary was the first dictionary to include *Ms.,* which it defined as "an abbreviation used as a title of courtesy before a woman's last name or before her given name and last name, whether she is married or not." By 1976 dictionaries published by Merriam-Webster, Random House, Doubleday, Funk & Wagnalls, and Collins-World also included *Ms.* as an accepted social form analogous to *Mr.*

The opposition to *Ms.* has been intense and emotional, however. The arguments that it cannot be pronounced, that it has an ugly sound, or that it is not a true abbreviation are often offered with a vehemence not justified by their merit. Is it possible to tell by looking at *Mr.* and *Mrs.* that they are pronounced "mister" and "missiz" (or "mizz" in some parts of the country)? Is the sibilant in *Ms.* any more disagreeable to the ear than the hiss in *Miss*? For sheer silliness of sound one would be hard pressed to beat the long-accepted plural form of *Mr.*, commonly if inelegantly pronounced "messers." Finally, is *Ms.* any less true an abbreviation than *Miss* or *Mrs.*? If the problem is guilt by association with the opprobrious *mistress,* all three titles must share it.

In its earliest meaning *mistress* described a woman, either married or unmarried, who had authority over servants, children, or a household. It was a prestigious word, like *master,* and when prefixed to a woman's name was a title of respect. Some time in the seventeenth century the noun *mistress* and its written abbreviations *Mis., Miss,* and *Mrs.,* acquired the additional meaning of concubine and occasionally of prostitute. The only forms to escape this association were apparently those prefixed to proper names as courtesy titles, and these eventually acquired their own pronunciations distinct from "mistress." In this period *Mrs.* was applied to all adult women, *Miss* to female children. Among other examples the Oxford English Dictionary cites Samuel Pepys's diary entry of 1666, "Little Miss Davis did dance a jigg after the end of the play," and Tobias Smollett's observation of 1751 that "Mrs. Grizzle . . . was now in the thirtieth year of her maidenhood."

By the beginning of the nineteenth century, however, the titles were no longer being used to distinguish children from adults. They had become labels identifying marital status: *Mrs.* distinguished married women and the "infantine term *miss,*" as it was characterized in H. J. Todd's 1818 edition of Johnson's dictionary, was applied to unmarried adult women as well as to children.[30]

No comprehensive study has been made of what prompted this change, but the timing strongly suggests a connection with women's increasing participation in the Industrial Revolution. The period was one of social ferment. Up to the time that large numbers of women left their homes to work in the new industries, the ordinary woman's primary identity had been that of daughter or wife/mother. She lived and worked under the roof of the man who ruled her person—her father or husband—and her relationship to him was apparent or easily learned. Once women gained a measure of independence as paid laborers, these ties were obscured and loosened. A man could not tell by looking at a woman spinning cotton in a textile mill to whom she "belonged" or whether she was "available."

Under these circumstances a simple means of distinguishing married from unmarried women was needed (by men) and it served a double purpose: it supplied at least a modicum of information about a woman's sexual availability, and it applied not so subtle social pressure toward marriage by lumping single women with the young and inexperienced. Attached to anyone over the age of about eighteen, *Miss* came in time to suggest the unattractive or socially undesirable qualities associated with such labels as "old maid" and "spinster" or the dreadful word *barren.* So the needs of patriarchy were served when a woman's availability for her primary role as helper and sexual partner was made an integral part of her identity—in effect, a part of her name.

Ironically, women's availability titles are often described in secretaries' manuals and books of etiquette as "courtesy titles" or "titles of respect" comparable to *Mr.* The sham of such descriptions was ingenuously exposed in the 1962 edition of *The New York Times Style Book for Writers and Editors,* still in print in 1976 and used by individuals and institutions throughout the country (though the *Times* had periodically amended its own rules, including the one regulating the use of *Mr.*). Under the entry "Mr., Mrs., Miss," the 1962 style book devotes forty-two lines to the uses of *Mr.,* including the information that "In general, *Mr.* is not used with the full name. It is used in second references to men of good standing. In general again, *Mr.* is not used with the names of persons who have been convicted of crime or who have unsavory reputations known without question to be deserved." A few paragraphs further on the style book notes, "*Mrs.* and *Miss* are a different case. They are to be used for all females, reputable or not, since they are needed to denote marital status." Needed by men and welcomed by many women, for in our society the status conferred on a woman by marriage and proclaimed by the symbol Mrs. is potent magic.

To fans of the British television program "Upstairs, Downstairs" it came as a surprise that Mrs. Bridges, the Bellamys' cook, had never been married. As Mr. Hudson, the butler, explained, "The title Mrs. is the usual honorarium enjoyed by cooks of a certain class," and one suddenly became aware of how differently this woman might have been perceived at 165 Eaton Place—as well as in East Orange and West Los Angeles—had she been known throughout the series as "Miss Bridges."

The frank statement, "I like my status as Mrs. too much to part with it,"[31] sums up the good-humored "call me Madam" attitude of many women who dislike *Ms.* To others, though, *Ms.* is an anathema, suggesting frightening visions of man-hating "women's libbers." Some speakers and writers use *Ms.* only as a putdown, either coyly or with contempt for the concept it represents. George Gilder, in a book criticizing the women's movement, appears to apply the title only to feminists with whom he disagrees most sharply, among them Mary Jane Sherfey, M.D., who comes out Ms. rather than Dr. Sherfey.[32] At a hearing on the New York State Equal Rights amendment, an opposition speaker addressing Senator Karen Burstein, an ERA supporter, began an agitated digression on whether to call her Miss, Mrs., or Ms.—a tactic Burstein quietly diverted by suggesting, "Perhaps it would be easier if you addressed me as Senator."[33]

In the first issue of *Ms.* magazine, published in the spring of 1972, the editors explained their choice of the publication's title: "Ms. is being adopted as a standard form of address by women who want to be recognized as individuals, rather than being identified by their relationship with a man." With the success of the magazine addressed to these women, "Ms." found increasing acceptability.

In 1973 the Government Printing Office sanctioned *Ms.* as an "optional prefix" for use in all federal government publications. Swimming against the stream, the governor of New Hampshire sent out a memo in 1974 to all secretaries employed by that state ordering that "the practice of using Ms. instead of Miss or Mrs. is to be discontinued immediately." The ruling was made, according to news reports, because the governor did not "believe" in the usage; what New Hampshire women felt about the matter he seems not to have considered germane.[34]

The *New York Times,* which covered the New Hampshire governor's edict without comment, was continuing to use either *Mrs.* or *Miss* for all women, but it had made a significant policy change in its use of *Mr.* In 1973 the paper announced it would no longer delete *Mr.* before the name of a man convicted of a crime because "we would be stripping him of his dignity in the pages of The Times." Managing Editor A. M. Rosenthal was asked if this meant the newspaper's acceptance of *Ms.* could be far behind. His answer, "Yes,"[35] appears to have left copy editors of the daily editions in something of a quandary (for example, Betty Friedan once appeared as "Mrs." on page 36 and as "Miss" on page 46 in the same issue),[36] but more important, it raised the question of basic courtesy. Having reported that Billie Jean King prefers to be known as Ms. King, the *Times* continued to call her Mrs. King.[37] In contrast, the paper has frequently referred to Henry Kissinger, who holds a Ph.D., as Dr. Kissinger, an unusual procedure unless the person referred to has indicated such a preference. And it consistently uses the African names that a number of prominent black men have adopted. The latter observance prompted journalist Ellen Cohn to remark that the *Times* editors "are misinformed about their own motivations.

The use of Ms. is not a question of style. It is a political matter. I am certain that if Eleanor Holmes Norton, who calls herself Ms. but whom the *Times* identifies as Mrs. as well as the chair*man* of New York City's Human Rights Commission, were to change her name to reflect African antecedents—the *Times* would take no notice."[38]

Other newspapers have been less lordly—at least to the point of going along with a woman's preference if they know it. In a conciliatory if paternalistic editorial, the *New Haven Register* announced the adoption of such a policy: "We understand the impatient feminist argument that all men share the common social title of 'Mister,' while the traditional women's titles, 'Mrs.' and 'Miss,' vary solely because of the woman's legal relationship to a man. But it is still a fact that many women, probably still a majority, cherish the legal relationship as a symbol of their personal ties to a man—or their independence of such ties—and find the married, unmarried distinctions not only bearable but desirable."[39] An indication, perhaps, of how strong a hold patriarchy still has on women's sense of identity.

Today, when one out of two marriages ends in divorce and many women choose to keep their birth names after marriage, titles purporting to indicate marital status are notably unreliable. The news media cannot possibly discover the title preferences of every woman in the news. Ultimately, the solution may be to dispense with social titles altogether for both women and men, and many writers and publications appear to be moving in that direction.

Ambrose Bierce was an early protester against social titles, and a perceptive one. In *The Devil's Dictionary,* published in 1906, he defined *Miss* as "a title with which we brand unmarried women to indicate that they are in the market. Miss, Missis (Mrs.), and Mister (Mr.) are the three most distinctly disagreeable words in the language, in sound and sense. . . . In the general abolition of social titles in this our country, they miraculously escaped to plague us. If we must have them let us be consistent and give one to the unmarried man. I venture to suggest *Mush,* abbreviated to *Mh.*"

After the anonymous inventor of *Ms.* had moved in the other direction, and the idea of one, all-purpose female title began to take hold, satirists revived Bierce's suggestion that what was needed was a new title for unmarried males. But now the idea was given a new twist: instead of consistency, the argument shifted to a woman's "right" to know a man's marital status: keep *Miss* and *Mrs.,* but split *Mr.* into similar titles indicating availability. Theodore M. Bernstein suggested *Bar* for bachelors and *Wow* for widowers,[40] and Russell Baker came up with *Murm* for married men, *Smur* for the unmarried. Baker was full of sympathy:

> Miss Petacci, being introduced to the dark and enchanting man with the smoldering eyes, is infinitely better served with an introduction that goes, "Miss Petacci, may I introduce Murm Carlo Lovborg," than she would be with, "Miz Petacci, Mister Lovborg."
>
> On the instant, "Miss" Petacci has vital information of the sort that women need on the instant in these hectic times. . . . Even if you encounter only fifty people a week, you are as sunk as a camel in the Everglades if you need hours, days, months, even a disaster to obtain the basic data required to determine whether you want to have anything to do with them.[41]

Baker is a funny writer, and this was a funny column, except that it ended on a bitter note: "It is the truth, women yearning for liberation, that will set you free. 'Miz' sets us all back a little further in an age already darkening."

Somehow one hears in those doleful phrases the melancholy, long, withdrawing roar that fell on Matthew Arnold's ear a century ago. We do live in a darkening age, as women and men both know; so let us be true to one another. Whether or not Ms. Petacci and Mr. Lovborg are or were or will be married—to each other or to someone else—has nothing to do with setting us forward or back.

At a federal hearing on discrimination against women, Dr. Pauli Murray, lawyer, teacher, and eventually an ordained priest in the Episcopal Church, called ridicule of women "the psychic counterpart of violence against blacks." Speaking to fellow journalists, Ellen Cohn reiterated a point that others have also made: sexism is the only form of bigotry still treated as good clean fun by the American press. Women are beginning to look at what lies behind the ridicule, the mocking bigotry, the endless derisive stereotypes. "Women have been made to look ridiculous for too long," said Stephanie Harrington. "And men have had reasons for wanting women to look ridiculous. Women humorists ought to start focusing on what is ridiculous about those reasons."[42]

Chapter 7

What Is Woman?

In English many more words associated with women have sexual connotations than have words associated with men. This is not surprising in the context of our culture, nor is it surprising that women tend to speak in a more deferential, uncertain manner than men. Both these linguistic circumstances developed because in a patriarchy sexuality is seen as the primary reason for a woman's existence. Women and sexuality are equated; men are understood to exist for "higher things." Put another way, women are perceived as sexual beings who occasionally think, men as rational beings for whom procreational sex is a duty and recreational sex a source of relief from the burdens of running the world. In the words of the aphoristic Otto Weininger, "Man possesses sexual organs; her sexual organs possess woman."[1]

Weininger was not trying to be funny. When he said, "Woman is nothing but sexuality . . . she is sexuality itself," he was putting into words a pervasive if rarely expressed view, which may explain the popularity of his book *Sex and Character*, first published in Vienna in 1903 and widely reprinted. (The latest American edition came out in 1988.) Weininger's Viennese contemporary, the renowned psychiatrist Alfred Adler, was one of the few thinkers developing in the early years of the twentieth century to break through the accepted stereotypical view of women. "All our institutions, our traditional attitudes, our laws, our morals, our customs, give evidence of the fact that they are determined and maintained by privileged males for the glory of male domination," Adler wrote. ". . . That woman must be submissive, is an unwritten but deeply rooted law. . . ."[2]

One result of this deeply rooted law requiring women's submission is a double standard of linguistic behavior. "Proper" language has long been the mark of what is called femininity, but as some women have always known, its restrictive effects are as hobbling in their way as overrefinements of dress have been inhibiting in theirs. In 1736 one such anonymous woman protested in verse the greater freedom of speech enjoyed by men in colonial Virginia:

They plainly can their Thoughts disclose
Whilst ours must burn within:
We have got Tongues, and Eyes, in Vain,
And Truth from us is Sin.

* * * *

Then Equal Laws let Custom find,
And neither Sex oppress;
More Freedom give to Womankind,
Or give to Mankind less.[3]

Alas, as she might have said, more than two hundred and fifty years later women are still shackled by custom's unequal laws, a state of affairs demonstrated by two unrelated news events in the spring of 1974. On April 23 of that year the Appellate Division of New Jersey's Superior Court upheld the dismissal of a public school teacher, Kathleen Pietrunti, for "improper conduct" and the use of "abusive rhetoric" in a speech she had made three years earlier as president of a local teachers' association. The court ruled that Pietrunti had violated "minimum professional standards" by making "unladylike and unfeminine" remarks about school board officials. Only one example was reported in the *New York Times* coverage of the decision: it was Pietrunti's reference to the head of the school board, one William Bell, as "Ding Dong Bell."[4]

A week later in Washington the Government Printing Office began public distribution of the edited transcripts of Oval Office conversations related to Watergate, and within hours "expletive deleted" had become part of our national vernacular. A large segment of the news media and the public, having filled in the blanks with educated guesses, expressed their outrage. Others, though disturbed, felt that the President's language was relatively inconsequential compared to the enormity of the undeleted information the transcripts also disclosed.

The circumstances of these two events differed greatly, of course. One involved the President of the United States and the other a local schoolteacher, and the remarks in one case were made in private whereas Pietrunti was speaking in a semipublic meeting—an orientation session for seventy-five newly employed teachers. But if one mentally reverses the sexes of the speakers involved, the irrelevance of the circumstances becomes clear. American citizens might have been even more shocked to learn that a woman who had been elected their Chief Executive used ribald and profane language, but the context would have remained much the same—part of even greater shock over the abuse of power and disdain for the people and their Constitution the taped conversations revealed. But if the male president of a local teachers' association had referred to school board president Wilma Bell as "Ding Dong Bell," the incident would have been treated as a joke. Even if he had called the school board president a "mental midget," as Pietrunti did on another occasion, or referred to the superintendent of schools as a "villain" (as she also did), it is doubtful if he would have received more than a slap on the wrist. Kathleen Pietrunti, a tenured teacher with seventeen years of experience and an exemplary record, lost her job.[5] (So did Richard Nixon, but not, it need hardly be added, for "abusive rhetoric.")

As in eighteenth-century Virginia, girls and boys in America today are still brought up to speak differently. Although this double standard is beginning to give way—mainly because women in growing numbers are ignoring it—the punishment society imposes on women for linguistic rebellion can still be severe, as the Pietrunti case showed. When small boys swear and use other rough forms of speech, their behavior, for better or worse, is at least tolerated, if not condoned as appropriate. They are trying to be like men, people say. Similarly, when men pepper their conversation with expletives, they are excused on the grounds that "boys will be boys." After the Watergate tapes had been published, a Frank Williams cartoon in the *Detroit Free Press* showed a little boy sitting on the floor with some blocks and a ball—frustrated and enraged. We know he is swearing because in the old "Jiggs" tradition the balloon issuing from his mouth is filled with exploding stars and squiggles. Looking on are a nonplussed woman and a laughing man who says, "He may grow up to be President!"[6]

Little girls are not permitted such freedom. Verbally as well as in their physical actions they are expected to be more restrained and considerate than boys, and in time these expectations affect the speech patterns of both sexes. Males adopt a more direct, forceful way of talking, females a more tentative, questioning approach. What one typically phrases as a statement or command the other is apt to formulate as a request.

Jill Volner, a Justice Department lawyer who became prominent as an assistant prosecutor during the Watergate trials, put the situation this way: "If I were to act like a man in a courtroom, the jury wouldn't accept me—yelling and shouting, as some of the lawyers in the Watergate case did, are not acceptable in women. It's far more effective for me to be quiet and ask questions than it is for me to get in a fight with a witness."[7] More effective both with a jury and with the rest of a society that insists her role as a woman must take precedence over her role as an attorney. But what of the woman whose temperament chafes at that priority? Must it always be assumed that a woman whose verbal style is self-assertive is acting like a man?

One woman who never accepted that assumption deftly nailed its implication in an interview on William Buckley's television series "Firing Line." After an introduction in which Buckley spoke with genuine admiration of the achievements of his guest, Clare Boothe Luce, the following exchange took place:

> BUCKLEY: I should like to begin by asking her whether she finds implicit condescension in the rhetorical formulations with which men tend to introduce her.
>
> LUCE: Bill, I thank you for that warm and extraordinarily friendly introduction. You'll be pleased to know that in the entire introduction, which was flattering, to say the least, there was only one masculine put-down. This is a high level of achievement for a man introducing a woman.
>
> You spoke of her inability, on occasions, to hold her tongue. Now, had you been speaking of a man who spoke out and made enemies for himself in the process, whether he was speaking out stupidly or rightly, wrongly, you would have said, "He is blunt. He makes enemies by what he says. He is overly candid." You might have used many phrases. But the phrase "hold her tongue" is a phrase that men frequently use about children and women.
>
> BUCKLEY: Sort of comes out of *Taming of the Shrew*?
>
> LUCE: No, it comes out of man's desire, highly successful, through the centuries to master women. One of the first things children and women are taught to do is to hold their tongues.[8]

Hold their tongues and speak deferentially. Robin Lakoff, a linguist at the University of California at Berkeley, has done significant work on the effect "women's language"—including the way women are expected to speak—has in establishing and maintaining our society's concept of "woman's place."[9] The purpose of this special language, Lakoff postulates, is to submerge a woman's personal identity. Discouraged from expressing herself forcefully, a girl may acquire speech habits that communicate uncertainty, hesitancy, indecisiveness, and subordination.

Among the devices Lakoff cites as typical of women's language is the tag question. Rather than making a simple strong statement—"War is terrible," for example—a woman might say, "War is terrible, isn't it?" giving the impression that she is unsure of her opinion, is reluctant to state it flat out, and is asking for confirmation. Another pattern found only among women, Lakoff observes, is a speaker's use of the rising inflection that indicates she is asking a question when actually she is giving an answer. In reply to "When will dinner be ready?" for example, she may say, "Oh—around six o'clock?" as though adding "if that's okay with you, if you agree." Again, the effect is that the speaker is unsure of herself, unable to make up her mind, and not to be trusted with real responsibility.

Lakoff points out that by seeming to leave decisions open and not imposing a viewpoint on others, women's language comes off sounding more polite than men's. As a tag question is a kind of polite statement, a request is a polite command that does not force obedience. So where a man might say, "Please close the door," or "Close the door," a woman is more apt to say, "Will you please close the door?" or "Won't you close the door?" suggesting in either case that the decision is up to the person addressed rather than to the speaker.

Most women in our society are socialized to use women's language to a greater or lesser degree, Lakoff believes, and their use of this language is then turned against them:

> If the little girl learns her lesson well, she is not rewarded with unquestioned acceptance on the part of society; rather, the acquisition of this special style of speech will later be an excuse others use to keep her in a demeaning position, to refuse to take her seriously as a human being. . . . So a girl in this situation is damned if she does, damned if she doesn't. If she refuses to talk like a lady, she is ridiculed and subjected to criticism as unfeminine; if she does learn, she is ridiculed as unable to think clearly, unable to take part in a serious discussion: in some sense, as less than fully human.[10]

Both these choices—to be less than a woman or less than a person—are, as Lakoff says, highly painful. Males are not required to make a similar choice. Having learned the lesson of his male peers, a man "is at once accepted as a man and as a fully functioning member of human society." He is not, like a woman, denied the means of expressing himself strongly and directly. Thus the effect on males and females of disparate linguistic training, Lakoff concludes, "is that the latter group is systematically denied access to power, on the grounds that its members are not capable of holding it."[11]

The phenomenon of "women's language" is not limited to Western societies. It is apparently directly related to the almost universal judgment that women are inferior to men—a judgment arrived at by the male definers of what constitutes "superiority" and accepted by many females who obligingly behave as though the judgment were true. Gunnar Myrdal, in an appendix to his major work on racism, *An American Dilemma,* compared the status of Western women as a class with that of American blacks: both groups have traditionally been assigned a "place" in a society dominated by white males[12] and both acquired traits, like submissiveness and self-deprecation, that helped to keep them there.

In addition to subservient patterns of speech, girls and

women also tend, in many cultures, to use more "correct" grammar and pronunciation than boys and men. The linguist Mary Ritchie Key, commenting on this behavior in her book *Male/Female Language,* says: "Apparently females attempt some kind of equilibrium by reaching a higher status in language to compensate for their lower status as members of society. . . . Linguists who do field work have noted that dialect differences and unusual forms of speech may be difficult to elicit from women who are more socially conscious of being denigrated. Language is one way in which females can better themselves, even if only in their own image."[13]

A linguistic counterpart of delicately crooking the little finger when drinking tea? If one is forbidden to take part in a world that matters, one overrefines what remains. But the same coin, in reverse, may explain why, once members of an oppressed class begin to rebel against their oppression, the old linguistic restraints are among the first to be challenged.

In the early 1920s, Otto Jespersen wrote about differences between the speech of British women and men in his book *Language: Its Nature Development and Origin.* Today the examples he used sound unreal:

> Among the things women object to in language must be specially mentioned anything that smacks of swearing; where a man will say "He told an infernal lie," a women [*sic*] will rather say, "He told a most dreadful fib." Such euphemistic substitutes for the simple word 'hell' as 'the other place,' 'a very hot' or 'a very uncomfortable place' probably originated with women. They will also use *ever* to add emphasis to an interrogative pronoun, as in "Whoever told you that?" or "Whatever do you mean?" and avoid the stronger 'who the devil' or 'what the dickens.' For surprise we have the feminine exclamations 'Good gracious,' 'Gracious me,' 'Goodness gracious,' 'Dear me' by the side of the more masculine 'Good heavens,' 'Great Scot.'[14]

In 1933, eleven years after Jespersen published these observations, the restraints that had governed socially acceptable language in the nineteenth and early twentieth centuries began to give way. In December of that year Judge John M. Woolsey ruled that the ban on the importation into the United States of James Joyce's *Ulysses* should be lifted. Of this decision Morris L. Ernst, who represented Random House in the court action, wrote: "The *Ulysses* case marks a turning point. . . . The necessity for hypocrisy and circumlocution in literature has been eliminated. Writers need no longer seek refuge in euphemisms. They may now describe basic human functions without fear of the law."[15]

The subsequent proliferation of formerly taboo words appearing in print and speech might not have surprised Jespersen. But he would probably have been startled that women were in the vanguard of those who broke the barriers in print. With her customarily thorough research, Ethel Strainchamps produced the following particulars, which she attributes to the fact that women lack "the galvanic response of males" to forbidden sex words and so are freer to disregard the taboos against them.

> Three of the first authors of international standing to use the word *fuck* in their books after the courts made it legally permissible were women: Iris Murdoch, Doris Lessing, and Carson McCullers. Many more probably had it edited out of their manuscripts by timorous male editors. In Sybille Bedford's report of the *Lady Chatterley* obscenity trial, where the taboo words were discussed in detail, *Esquire,* "the magazine for men," let all the other words stand but substituted "that word" for *fuck. Playboy,* more aggressively all-male used an *f* and three dashes to represent the word as it was spoken by Helen Gurley Brown in an interview. Mrs. Brown had been asked if she had had any difficulty with editors in getting *Sex and the Single Girl* into print as she wrote it. She replied that the only serious contretemps occurred when

> she discovered in the galleys that *Frig you!* had been substituted for *Fuck you!* as the proper retort by a young woman to neighbors who criticized her for sleeping with a man she was not married to. Mrs. Brown said she was outraged and told the editor, "No lady would ever say that word!"[16]

Strainchamps herself, who may be the country's leading authority on the use of taboo words in print and who is surely its funniest, once wrote an article on her linguistic specialty that was rejected, with varying excuses, by *Harper's, Playboy,* and the *American Scholar.* Finally she sent the manuscript to the *Yale Review,* mentioning the previous rejections and the reasons given. This time the reply, which began, "At last you have found an honest editor," explained that the trouble she was having in getting the piece accepted was neither the subject matter nor the style, but the circumstance "that you are a woman writing on a subject which, according to contemporary mores, women do not write on."[17]

Fortunately, contemporary mores are changing, for the effect of the linguistic double standard was (and is) itself a double one: as long as what used to be called the language of the streets was suppressed because women were not supposed to hear it, it went unexamined and its implications were unacknowledged; and as long as women were shielded from it by being kept out of such all-male preserves as the press box, the machine shop, and the smoke-filled rooms where political decisions are made, they continued to be economically penalized. Now, as an indirect result of women's vocational gains, the language barrier is also being broken. And if the female presence in former male strongholds has not produced a great purifying of speech among the regulars, neither have the heavens fallen. As a blue-collar worker said of her aural environment when her grievance complaint finally led to a job on an assembly line where no woman had worked before, "It's not the swearing that bugs me. It's the constant apologies."[18] Women know the meanings of the words they are thought too delicate to hear, and some, of course, can blue the air as effectively as any man.

It is hard to pin down just how far attitudes about the so-called dirty words have changed in the last thirty or forty years. Each person's age and upbringing and individual point of view make a difference. Efforts to apply the United States Supreme Court's 1973 ruling on local control of obscenity in print and public performances show that in a country of more than two hundred million people, and even within communities of only a few thousand, these differences constitute a formidable mix. Children continue to startle their parents when they come home with vulgarisms they learned away from home; certain words—if they are printed at all—are still spelled with blanks or asterisks in newspapers and news magazines reporting on who said what to whom; television and radio continue to censor coarse language more stringently than the periodicals; and a lot of people who think of themselves as healthily uninhibited can still get an unexpected jolt from some of the language used in popular books, films, and plays. At least two generalizations are warranted, however: most dictionaries have dropped the pretense that formerly forbidden words do not exist; and women use words, both publicly and in private, their mothers would not have used or even understood only a few decades ago.[19]

Society, of course, still censures women more harshly than men for using "improper" language, and probably many more women than men continue to shy away from words they themselves identify as blasphemous or vulgar. But today the whole question of verbal obscenity is out in the open. It can be looked at for what it is—the degradation of human beings, particularly of women. In her introduction to *An Intelligent Woman's Guide to Dirty Words,* a compilation of terms used to describe women, one of the compilers, Ruth Todasco, says, "I have finally begun to perceive what the English language says *to* me and *about* me."

It is not a pretty picture, for as Todasco observes,

"Women's sexuality has been so tortured by patriarchy that the language does not exist to describe her sexual needs without prejudice to her person."[20] In fifty pages of definitions culled from established dictionaries, the guide "wrenches the English language from its centuries-old degrading complacencies about women." As thus presented, woman in our language is a sickening image: woman as object, woman as man has named and defined her.

Among other things, the guide documents from standard dictionaries the extraordinary fact that with the possible exception of *female,* the everyday words for a female person have acquired either directly or in combinations the additional meaning of "prostitute": *woman of the streets, fancy woman, fruitwoman, fallen woman; girl, girlie, call girl, joy girl, bad girl, working girl; lady of pleasure, lady of the evening.* Like *mistress,* the titles *queen, madam,* and *dame* all have debased meanings unmatched by masculine-gender counterparts.

The guide lists words for animals that are applied to women, such as *bat* ("prostitute," "an unattractive usually unpleasant woman") and *dog* ("a woman inferior in looks, character, or accomplishments; sometimes: prostitute"); and words for foods such as *chicken* ("a young woman of easy familiarity"), *mutton* ("a loose woman; a prostitute"), and *tart* ("a wanton or loose girl or woman; esp. prostitute"). It lists terms for parts of the body that become, by transference, words for women themselves. One section is devoted to stereotypes like *bathing beauty, glamour girl, harpy,* and *wallflower* that define by male standards who is attractive and who is a failure. Eighty-nine entries relate to woman as "whore" and another hundred and twenty-nine to woman as "whorish." For as women have discovered, Todasco says,

> words meaning whore apply to any woman, single or married, employed or unemployed, high, low, or middle class, who offends or appeals sexually to male sensibilities. A lady who makes men uncomfortable about themselves is no

> longer a lady, as by definition a lady is a woman bred to please. Both a lady and a whore are supposed to give men what they think they want in the way they want it. A woman is put into one category or the other depending on the male's perception of his own need and comfort. For that reason, a woman testifying to rape is automatically regarded by men as whore, as having asked for what she gets. Their presumption that man is the natural protector of woman makes it painful if not impossible for them to admit that women are victims of deliberate male violence.[21]

Knowing themselves to be neither whore nor madonna but inseparable mixtures, like men, of mind and body, women are "pinned in ambivalence," she says, forced to deny their sexuality or trade on it.

Among the vulgarisms used to define women sexually, some are so common they slip out as though innocent of offense. When a television newscaster, speaking of foreign travel, said on the air she would do such-and-such if she were abroad, her male co-anchor punned casually, "But you *are* a broad."[22] This popular epithet may even be used with the intent to praise. The book jacket of *Exclusive!* by Marilyn Baker, a reporter who covered the Patricia Hearst story, says of the author, "The ultimate tribute about her work came from the FBI agent in charge of the case: 'I wish to God we had that broad's connections.' "

Sexual terms too explicit for use on the air or on book jackets define women genitally and sometimes anally as well. Barbara Lawrence, writing in *Redbook,* drew attention to the latter: expressions like "piece of tail," she pointed out, suggest that "there is no significant difference between the female channel through which we are all conceived and born and the anal outlet common to both sexes—a distinction that pornographers have always enjoyed obscuring."[23]

Discussing the implications of sexual obscenity, Lawrence, professor of humanities at the State University of New York at

Old Westbury, went on to say, "This effort to deny women their biological identity, their individuality, their humanness, is such an important aspect of obscene language that one can only marvel at how seldom, in an era preoccupied with definitions of obscenity, this fact is brought to our attention." Critics, teachers, and writers, she notes, are often reluctant today to admit that they are angered or shocked by obscenity. "Bored, maybe, unimpressed, aesthetically displeased, but—no matter how brutal or denigrating the material—never angered, never shocked. And yet how eloquently angered, how piously shocked many of these same people become if denigrating language is used about any minority group other than women; if the obscenities are racial or ethnic, that is, rather than sexual."[24]

Words used to insult men differ in several ways from those used to insult women. In the first place, there are not as many. Scatological terms and the milder epithets that question someone's intelligence or integrity, like *blockhead* and *fink,* are directed at women too. Terms for male animals like *bull* and *buck* usually carry the implication of sexual prowess, whereas *cow, vixen, bitch,* and the like imply passivity or bad temper, and often promiscuity as well. *Womanizer, Don Juan,* and *stud* can be taken as compliments (at women's expense), and the cutting edge of *pimp, panderer,* and *procurer* comes from their association with female prostitutes: to imply that a man lives off the earnings of women is a special insult in men's eyes. *Beast, brute, lecher,* and *dirty old man* are mild epithets, almost Victorian in tone if not in implication. Ironically, the word *rapist* is not considered an obscenity.

Slang terms for the testes are sometimes used as negative or disapproving exclamations, but one such term is a common synonym for courage and toughness, as in the bumper sticker slogan, "It takes leather balls to play soccer." No such positive connotations attach to *prick,* but even this word does not convey the absolute scorn of *slit, slot, snatch,* and *gash. Cunt,* when used contemptuously of either a woman or a man, is consummate abuse.

Son of a bitch and *bastard* both shift the onus onto women, the first completely, the second at least in part. The newer expletive *motherfucker* is to many people among the most obscene of the current terms used to insult men because it exploits the deepest of sexual taboos, but here again it is a woman who is ultimately degraded as the object of abuse.

It could be that male-gender obscenities are less numerous than their female counterparts because women have been socialized to suppress their rage at being sexually victimized by men and so have not developed a comparable vocabulary with which to retaliate. The more probable reason is that the ultimate insults males direct at each other are those expressed in female-gender terms. One small boy humiliates another by calling him "a sissy" or "a girl," and among adults "effeminate" and "womanish" are offensive, if polite, descriptives. Ethel Strainchamps comments that militant blacks would have riled white males far more effectively by calling them "females" rather than "honkies," but citing the "fraternal bond among males that cuts across even class and race lines," she concludes, it "would have been too low a blow."[25] This was the bond Bobby Seale broke when he taunted Judge Julius Hoffman at the conspiracy trial of the Chicago Eight by shouting, "You're just a woman!"—the insult Judge Hoffman was said to have resented more than any other.[26]

In an article on male professional athletes, the writer Clayton Riley spelled out the nature of this kind of insult more fully:

> The American male athlete's attitude about women . . . can be summed up in a single word: pussy. Not simply because athletes believe they should get plenty as part of the divine-right-of-kings principle by which most of them live, but because athletes so disdain the thought of being women. The worst thing you can call another athlete is a "pussy." The thought of being a woman so terrifies most American males, athletes and nonathletes alike, that any other condi-

> tion seems preferable—even death, which can at least be considered an "honorable" state.[27]

One remembers psychologist Ruth Hartley's observation that for many boys growing up in America, "the scramble" to escape the "womanly" things they must *not* be "takes on all the aspects of panic, and the outward semblance of non-femininity is achieved at a tremendous cost of anxiety and self-alienation."[28]

One of the favorite words used to disparage women became an issue in a sex discrimination case brought by a New Jersey woman. The hearing examiner asked both sides to present legal briefs addressed to the question "whether use of the word 'bitch' by a male in reference to a woman carries any inference of bias or prejudice against women." Abundant legal authority exists to the effect that when an individual woman is called a bitch the intent is to derogate her, but the implication of bias against women in general had never before been put to a legal test.[29]

In technical use, a bitch is a female dog or other canine capable of estrus and gestation, two stages in which certain behavioral as well as physiological mechanisms are essential for reproduction. A dog in heat actively seeks insemination; judged by our cultural standards, the dog is "lewd," and according to standard dictionaries that is one of the meanings the word *bitch* is assigned when applied to a woman. During gestation, a canine develops a pattern of defensive and offensive behavior that increases after she gives birth; again, by prevailing human standards she may be said to be spiteful, malicious, unpleasant, and selfish to the point of stopping at nothing to reach her goal (which is to protect her offspring). According to standard dictionaries all these meanings can also be implied when the word is used of a female person.

Drawing on these facts, the complainant and her counsel argued that the word *bitch* conveys the same connotative meanings when used of a woman that it does when used of a dog and that in using the word the speaker "betrays a preconceived judgment that a woman's behavior is directed by her reproductive function; the word repudiates her for want of docility to the male." Therefore, they said, the use of the word "does manifest prejudice and a discriminatory attitude toward women as a group . . . and, conversely, betrays prejudice toward the woman of whom it is said because of her sex."[30] The hearing examiner agreed.

Sometimes the law seems to belabor the obvious, and yet it is possible to argue that *bitch* should not be regarded as a derogatory word, but a complimentary one, no matter what those who use it intend to the contrary. John may think Mary is a bitch because she is aggressive, but since he would praise the same quality in James, his use of *bitch* is in fact a compliment. This is the point of a feminist tract called "The Bitch Manifesto." As it is customarily used, the manifesto says, *bitch* "is a popular derogation to put down uppity women. . . . Like the term 'nigger,' 'bitch' serves the social function of isolating and discrediting a class of people who do not conform to the socially accepted patterns of behavior." But since socially accepted patterns are not necessarily the best or only ways of behaving, *bitch* can be a synonym for the woman who has a well-developed sense of pride and self-affirmation:

> Bitches are good examples of how women can be strong enough to survive even the rigid, punitive socialization of our society. As young girls it never quite penetrated their consciousness that women were supposed to be inferior to men in any but the mother/helpmate role. They asserted themselves as children and never really internalized the slave style of wheedling and cajolery which is called feminine.[31]

Groups of feminists who choose to call themselves witches want to rehabilitate that word in much the same way. Predictably, *wizard,* a masculine-gender counterpart of *witch* (the words come from the Old English *wicca* and *wicce*), has lost most of its negative connotations. "He is a financial wizard" is praise without aspersion, but much more than financial acumen was implied when Hetty Green was called the Witch of Wall Street.

Although *witch* may regain the prestige of one of its former meanings—a woman whose gifts included the power to heal—*bitch* has certain phonetic qualities that make it an unlikely candidate for rehabilitation. It can be spat out in such a way that anyone within earshot whose native tongue is English will recognize it as an epithet of disgust, whether or not they have ever heard it before. Similarly, Ethel Strainchamps has pointed out, all the dirtiest English taboo words combine speech and gesture; they are not purely arbitrary symbols. Each of these words, she notes, begins and ends with one of the blowing sounds—*k* or *c, f, p, s* or *sh,* and *t.* (The semiblowing sound *b* characterizes semidirty words.) As oral gestures of disgust, "they can no more be cleaned up by open and high-minded usage than can the Bronx cheer or the symbolic gestures of spitting and hawking." In the sound symbolism of these words, as in English generally, she says, the smaller vowels indicate smaller things and the large vowels, larger. Thus, "the word with *o* (as in *cock*) is the most impressive; the word with *u* (as in *cunt*) is the most nothing"—to which Strainchamps adds, "Men made the language."[32] (In this connection, Strainchamps has made the extraordinary discovery that the Great Vowel Shift—a series of changes in the pronunciation of vowels in English that began in the fourteenth century and is still going on—was not a purely capricious phenomenon, as linguists have hitherto supposed, but in personal nouns reflects sex and status associations.[33])

What gives this special class of obscene words their power is not what they mean (we use other words with the same meanings quite freely), but the disgust and violence they express phonetically. Therefore "there *is* a psychologically sound defense of the editorial reluctance to publish the English taboo words," Strainchamps says, and she points out that in the case of *fuck* and *cunt* the phonetic power can be extreme: "Their naked aggression and contempt betray facets of male attitudes toward women that civilized men prefer not to acknowledge."[34]

Since the potency of phonetically symbolic words lies partly in the way they are spoken, the detached, mechanical, or sometimes amorous use of these words defuses their violence. When an American in New Guinea asked an Australian soldier near the end of World War II how long he had been there, and the answer was "Oh, nineteen-forty fuckin'-two, fuckin'-three," the tone was not one of anger; just great weariness.[35] Spat out, the same word equates copulation with rape.

Yet a woman's use of the word *fuck* in that very context was a factor in convicting her of murder in the killing of a 300-pound man who, she testified, had helped his companion rape her. In the extensive press coverage of the trial of Inez Garcia in 1974, much attention was given to the defendant's psychological transformation from a demure wife and mother who had never been known to use strong language—a devout Catholic who had been too ashamed at first to tell anyone except her priest the reason why she had killed—to a woman who could shout from the witness stand, pounding her fists on the judge's bench, "I killed the motherfucker because I was raped!" In a grueling cross-examination she testified with tears streaming down her face as the prosecutor made her draw a diagram of the rape scene and describe how she was forced to undress by her attackers. "Then what happened?" the prosecutor asked. "You want me to tell you what happened after that?" "Yes." "He fucked me!" Garcia screamed.[36]

Some months later a university lecturer in creative writing, commenting on the case in a national magazine, said, "the defense of justifiable homicide in a state of shock and rage was undermined by Miss Garcia's foul-mouthed performance on the stand and her playing to the feminist gallery, as well as by the fact that the killing took place 17 minutes after the alleged rape occurred."[37] Seventeen minutes or seventeen years—the shock and rage of a woman or a man who has been raped is probably unspeakable, but Garcia's anguished use of *fuck* came close.

The taboo words of a language signal areas of psychic tension in the culture of its speakers. The prevalence of a particular genre of profanity is therefore thought by some experts to indicate either subconscious or unconscious anger or rebellion against an oppressive institution such as a dominating religion, a rigid standard of cleanliness, or a prudish code of sexual behavior.[38] American swearwords cover all these areas, perhaps reflecting our mixed heritage, but our most obscene verbal weapons also reveal the deep-seated, violent anger many men feel toward women. George Gilder provides a description of the official exploitation of this anger as it was once practiced at Paris Island, the Marine Corps boot camp:

> From the moment one arrives, the drill instructors begin a torrent of misogynistic and anti-individualist abuse. The good things are manly and collective; the despicable are feminine and individual. Virtually every sentence, every description, every lesson embodies this sexual duality, and the female anatomy provides a rich metaphor for every degradation.
>
> When you want to create a solidary group of male killers, that is what you do, you kill the women in them. That is the lesson of the Marines. And it works. . . .
>
> When the group leaves the Island and is once again exposed to the female body, it treats it, needless to say, as what is called a sexual object. . . . Pornographic movies near military centers tend to consist of violent attacks on women, and one of the favorite stories told on the return to the base from liberty is of the violent abuse of a whore.[39]

Why such a reservoir of hate exists to draw on is apparently related to the vicious cycle set up in any culture that divides the sexes into subject and object, aggressor and victim. This enormously complex subject has been probed by sociologists, anthropologists, clinical psychologists, and psychiatrists. Sociologist Nancy Chodorow summarizes in a few words one widely accepted view of the tragic, circular dilemma: "As long as women must live through their children, and men do not genuinely contribute to socialization and provide easily accessible models, women will continue to bring up sons whose sexual identity depends on devaluing femininity inside and outside themselves, and daughters who must accept this devalued position and resign themselves to producing more men who will perpetuate the system that devalues them."[40]

It is the theme Betty Friedan explored in *The Feminine Mystique.* "We need a drastic reshaping of the cultural image of femininity that will permit women to reach maturity, identity, completeness of self, without conflict with sexual fulfillment," she wrote. For "a woman who is herself only a sexual object lives finally in a world of objects, unable to touch in others the individual identity she lacks herself."[41]

To the degree that words, as we customarily use them, minimize the humanity of women and maximize their status as objects, we are all—females and males—the losers.

Chapter 8

The Specter of Unisex

"A unisex tongue would be a dull tongue—and a false one," E. B. White commented in a letter he wrote in 1974 to the author of a column on language and sexism published in the *San Francisco Chronicle.* The column was headed "A New English: Unbiased or Unsexed?" and in his letter White warned that many language crusaders "confuse sex difference with sex inequality." He agreed that language has played a role in reinforcing inequality, but, he said, "true inequality does not lie in our tongue, it lies in our hearts and in our habits, and language is remarkably sensitive to both."[1]

E. B. White was a writer's writer, a master of clarity and brevity who handled words with enviable grace. In his revised edition of William Strunk's *The Elements of Style* he wrote: "Style takes its final shape more from attitudes of mind than from principles of composition, for as an elderly practitioner once remarked, 'Writing is an act of faith, not a trick of grammar.' " And White went on, "This moral observation would have no place in a rule book were it not that style *is* the writer, and therefore what a man is, rather than what he knows, will at last determine his style."[2]

Every reader of *Charlotte's Web* knows that E. B. White, in his heart of hearts, had the makings of a feminist. But like many formally educated people who love the English language, he learned to speak and write it without realizing that it already is a unisex tongue. Its male orientation and use of subsuming masculine terms, for all their historic validity, no longer reflect reality, and so in this respect it is also a false tongue.

When White and others raise the specter of an unsexed or unisex tongue, they are confusing sex equality with sameness, sexual indifference, or absence of sex. Far from implying sameness, however, the language of equality emphasizes sexual differentiation by making women visible. Few women are asking to be called men, but more women than anyone has bothered to count are asking that they *not* be called men. They are asking that jobs and elected posts for which both men and women qualify be described by terms that include women, or at least do not exclude them.

This is the crux of the argument between those who, in their efforts to take gender out of the linguistic symbols for social realities that are not exclusively the province of either sex, offend those others who find neology repugnant both to the ear and to their sense of natural order. The latter see the question as one of aesthetics, the former as one of accuracy and politics.

Perhaps no word ruffles the purists more than *person,* especially when it is used to form compounds. "Thus, ad nauseum, chairperson, committeeperson, congressperson . . . ," writes a *Boston Globe* columnist. "Individuals who articulate this garbage are perceived to be au courant. It is a kind of sociological chic, like the tedious and uninspired obscenities and blasphemies of matrons."[3]

Professor Jacques Barzun of Columbia University, approaching the subject more coolly, suggests that the use of *person* is intended "to get rid of sex reference altogether, to confirm equality by insisting on our common humanness." With the last intention no one will quarrel, he said, but added, "The only question is whether it can be served so usefully by terminology that language has to be wrenched out of shape, on top of being misunderstood."[4]

Yes, answer those who opt for more accurate and inclusive words: equality can be usefully served by terminology. And no, they also say, we do not misunderstand: it is we who are keeping in touch with reality; you who are losing it. As for wrenching the language out of shape, almost all new terminology is awkward when it is first introduced. Give it a chance, and if the desire to affirm our common humanness is truly present, the right words to do the job will surface.

In the meantime, the very awkwardness of unfamiliar terminology can serve a purpose. Historian Ruth Schwartz Cowan, commenting on Barzun's criticism of *chairperson,* wrote, "The feminist rationale for that barbarous neologism (has there ever been a civilized neologism?) is neither linguistic nor esthetic—but purely political. *Chairperson* is deliberately meant to fall awkwardly off the tongue, because in its awkwardness it reminds us that persons in positions of authority may very well not be male."[5]

Not all backers of *-person* terms would agree with Professor Cowan's interpretation, but it may explain why all too frequently the companion of a *chairman* is a *chairperson,* not a *chairwoman.* One national voluntary organization, for example, in a newsletter announcing the names of members elected to its governing board, noted, "Board committee chairpersons are also identified"; in the list that followed, women were identified as chairpersons, men as chairmen.[6] Another group, the country's largest association of scientists, used the term *chairperson* consistently in announcing key appointments in a program concerned with opportunities in science for women and minorities, though elsewhere in the same publication higher posts were referred to as "chairman of the board" and "section chairmen."[7]

Television reporters and commentators provide almost endless examples that the logic involved in the *-person* ending is only vaguely grasped. In the news coverage of the 1974 Mitchell-Stans trial in New York, CBS newsman Robert Schakne said, when speaking of the jury, "The foreman—or, more accurately, the foreperson—of the jury is a young woman bank teller." The morning after the acquittal NBC newsmen Frank Blair and Robert Hager both referred to Sybil Kucharski as the jury's "forelady"; not wrong, but not quite right either, unless they would speak of a man as the jury's "foregentleman." Barbara Walters, who interviewed Kucharski on the NBC "Today Show," had no trouble: she used the term *forewoman,* an accurate description of the individual and a parallel to the more familiar, but in this case inappropriate, *foreman.*

A number of groups, having tried *chairperson* or *chair-one,* have solved the problem by dropping the suffix altogether. "We've gone through the chairperson bit and now we use just chair," as someone said not long ago, and perhaps that is where the matter will finally rest. The word *chair* already means "an office or position of authority or dignity," and "a person who holds such an office or position." Why be more complicated?

The State of Connecticut now has a law requiring that whenever the title of a public office denotes gender—as in chairman, councilman, alderman, or that respected New England post, selectman—the title shall suit the sex of the person holding the office. The initiator of the law, State Senator Betty Hudson, opposes the use of all sex-designating titles as a matter of principle. "An office holder's sex is irrelevant to the performance of the job," she points out, but "where such a title exists, it should suit the office holder. To call a woman a 'man' is not only unfair to the woman involved, but also denies to all women the recognition and regard which accrue from the achievements of members of their sex and attributes those achievements to the male sex."[8] After the law became effective in 1973 Hudson heard from a number of women in public office who did not want their titles changed. "That convinced me the bill was necessary," she says. "Some women obviously believed that being called 'selectwoman' instead of 'selectman' would diminish their position. The insidious thing about stereotyping is that the minority tends to start believing the stereotype themselves, and begins acting the way the majority expects them to."[9]

In California the argument that terms like "workmen's compensation" and masculine pronouns used generically "are part of the way the English language is used" was rejected by the people, who apparently felt that such reverence for the status quo was obsolete. In 1974 they voted to remove words like *congressmen, assemblymen,* and the pronouns *he, his,* and *him* from their Constitution entirely.[10]

Editorial decisions made by two leading scientific organizations also indicate a climate of change. In 1971, after sixty-five years of publication as *American Men of Science,* that prestigious directory of scientists was retitled *American Men and Women of Science;* and in 1973 the American Anthropological Association passed a resolution urging anthropologists "to become aware in their writing and teaching that their wide use of the term 'man' as generic for the species is conceptually confusing." The association further urged "that it be replaced by more comprehensive terms such as 'people' and 'human beings' which include both sexes."[11] What these straws in the wind seem to indicate is a linguistic trend away from unisex terminology and toward the recognition that two sexes not only exist but that they share a common humanity.

Legal cases in which an interpretation of *man* was at issue included one in Hampden County, Massachusetts. There a will setting up a scholarship fund "to aid and assist worthy and ambitious young men to acquire a legal education" was successfully challenged in 1975. A probate judge, ruling in favor of three women law students who had been denied assistance from the fund because of their sex, concurred in their argument that the word *men* in the will is generic and includes both sexes. The administrators of the fund disagreed and appealed the ruling.[12] Meanwhile in New York State a local Kiwanis Club brought suit against Kiwanis International whose board of trustees had revoked their charter because the branch had refused to exclude women from membership. The local club president explained, "We felt the words 'men' and 'man' in the bylaws in this day and age simply refer to persons male and female."[13]

Whatever the outcome of these and similar cases, they illustrate the futility of continuing to argue that the meaning of *man* is self-evident. As Mary Orovan noted in "Humanizing English," "The insidious thing is that woman can be included in man, or not, at the whim of the writer—or reader"—or by the judgment of a governing board, its legal counsel, or the courts.

"Humanizing English," an eight-page pamphlet first published in 1970, included Orovan's proposed common gender pronoun *co,* which was subsequently used in everyday speech and writing by members of several alternative-life-style communities. Twin Oaks Community, a group of some sixty adults and children living in Louisa, Virginia, adopted Orovan's nonsexist grammatical form in 1972. The pronoun later spread to other communities in Virginia and Missouri, was used in a book on radical therapy published in 1973 by Harper & Row, and routinely replaced "he or she" or "he/she" in the magazine *Communities,* addressed to cooperative-living groups across the country.

Orovan derived *co* from the Indo-European root form *ko,* the common ancestor of both the masculine and feminine

English pronouns. *Co,* with its suggestion of "together," is not used to replace either the masculine or feminine pronoun when applied to a specific individual, but only as an alternative to the unisex generic *he.* The Twin Oaks newsletter *Leaves,* for example, commented in an article on communal work undertaken by members, "Vacations are indeed a burden for the remaining members, but everyone takes cos turn at carrying the burden."[14]

Linguists insist that attempts to coin a common gender pronoun are doomed, and the failure of past efforts indicates they are right. The most long-lived coinage was proposed by the American composer Charles Converse in 1859.[15] *Thon,* which he derived as a contraction of "that one," was listed in Funk & Wagnalls New Standard Dictionary of 1913 with the examples "If Harry or his wife comes, I will be on hand to greet thon," and "Each pupil must learn thon's lesson"; and the term was still sufficiently recognized in 1959 to rate inclusion in the last printing of Webster's Second International. Another proposal included in the 1913 Funk & Wagnalls was *he'er*—with *his'er* and *him'er* as the possessive and objective forms—but although occasionally used, that suggestion had even less success than *thon.* Recent proposals, including *E, hesh, po, tey, ve, xe,* and *jhe,* have been more ephemeral still.

Yet new coinages keep coming, which suggests that the need for a common gender pronoun is deeply and sincerely felt. Efforts to get around the ambiguity or bias of *he* often end in a welter of *he-or-she*s. If to avoid that difficulty masculine pronouns are arbitrarily assigned in some categories and feminine pronouns in others, someone is bound to be displeased, as the authors of a manual for editorial freelancers admitted:

> At the risk of irritating male chauvinists, we have identified freelancers as "she," since the majority are female and the pronoun is handy. With the certain knowledge of irritating feminist activists, we have identified authors and editors as

> "he"—to differentiate them from "she." We hasten to acknowledge the numerous "he" freelancers and the many "she" editors and authors.[16]

The generic masculine pronouns can also thwart a writer's or speaker's intention when someone's identity is unknown or being kept secret. The famous gap in one of the Watergate tapes posed such a problem. After the explanation that the President's secretary had accidentally erased eighteen and a half minutes proved to be technically implausible, one expert examiner of the tape referred to the unknown person who had caused the repeated erasures as "he"—then quickly explained he had been using "the editorial 'he.' "[17] In another instance a newsman, reporting details of a jury's deliberations after it had returned a verdict, quoted a juror "who said that he or she did not want to be identified."[18] And sometimes the generic masculine usage is patently absurd: a bill introduced in a state legislature in 1975 would have required "that at least twenty-four hours before any abortion is performed in the state, the person who is to have such abortion shall receive counselling . . . concerning his decision to have such abortion."[19]

The decisive argument against using masculine terms generically, however, is not that they are often inadequate and sometimes ridiculous, but that they perpetuate the cultural assumption that the male is the norm, the female a deviation. It is this bias that the advocates of common gender terms want to eliminate. Yet almost every attempt to evolve new, amplifying symbols meets with hostility: the response of purists is sometimes so highly charged it is as though the male-is-norm assumption itself is what they are defending rather than the generic terms. And with almost knee-jerk predictability the name they invoke to support their views is that of George Orwell, who prophesied the demise of English and the advent of "Newspeak" in his novel *Nineteen Eighty-Four.*

Both the high level of emotion and the invocation of Orwell

were illustrated when students at the University of Tennessee decided in 1973 to try out the proposed common gender pronouns *tey, ter,* and *tem* in their newspaper, the *Daily Beacon.* The experiment was inaugurated in good faith and carefully explained. "To continue using 'he' as the common gender pronoun is to support the implication that women do not rate equal status with men," the paper said editorially, and it offered the following sentence as an example of when the new terms would be used: "A new chancellor will be appointed in late summer, but tey will take office in the fall after the University has given tem time to learn ter responsibilities."[20]

The experiment was scheduled to last for eight months, but it was dropped after only three in the face of misinterpretation, misunderstanding, and ridicule. A wire service news item, carried in newspapers across the country, reported that the *Beacon* was trying to avoid all references to sex.[21] Even more discouraging to the student editors was the response of critics within the university. "An asinine reflex of Women's Lib" and "a great leap forward into the nineteenth century" were typical. "Arrant nonsense," wrote a member of the Department of English. "The substitute 'words'—poor raped pronouns . . . [are] purely nonsense syllables of an ungracious, guttural Newspeak; masculine pronouns down the Memory Hole. . . ."[22]

George Orwell was a crusader against the abuse of English and, above all, a defender of precision. He looked on language "as an instrument for expressing and not for concealing or preventing thought."[23] Although he might not have liked the students' choice of pronouns (Orwell used "he" generically and did not question its ambiguity), he probably would have sympathized with their motives.

As the official language of the thought-controlled society Orwell described in *Nineteen Eighty-Four,* Newspeak was designed by its fictional creators to make any nonconforming ideas unthinkable. Although they accomplished their aim partly by inventing new words—the point most people today seem to remember when their circuitry flashes "Newspeak"—the chief devices the inventors of the new language used were to eliminate undesirable words like *peace* and *freedom,* to redefine the old words that remained, and to telescope names and phrases into a sort of verbal shorthand that diminished their previous meanings. The literature of the past, including Chaucer, Shakespeare, and Milton, was being translated into Newspeak so that the originals were "not merely changed into something different, but actually changed into something contradictory of what they used to be."[24]

The intention of feminists who want to counteract the sexist nature of English (including the student editors at the University of Tennessee) is exactly the opposite: they are trying to make English more precise, to make it say what it means rather than conceal meaning. The objective of Newspeak, as Orwell explained with emphasis, was "not to extend but to *diminish* the range of thought."[25] Since the objective of feminists is not to diminish but to *extend* the range of thought, those who accuse them of Newspeak are either misreading Orwell or misreading the women's movement.

George Orwell's understanding of the power of language is deeply relevant to the University of Tennessee experiment and to the women's movement itself. Clearly the *Beacon* editors, unlike their critics, were trying to open the mind's eye to all the options possible. As the students were aware, to refer to the university's future and still unidentified chancellor as *he* could not help but foster the image of a male appointee. What they proposed was not to eliminate masculine gender pronouns, as their detractor in the English department somehow imagined. It was to permit the unambiguous use of all pronouns: *he* for a male, *she* for a female, and a third, open, liberating form when circumstances preclude being specific.

When *Time* magazine attacked feminist linguistic concerns in a full-page essay, the author, who also called upon the name of Orwell, coined the term Sispeak and, as many others have done, telescoped the phrase Women's Liberation to Women's Lib.[26] (Some reduce it to FemLib.) "It was perceived," Orwell explained of such thinking, "that in thus abbreviating a name one narrowed and subtly altered its meaning, by cutting out most of the associations that would otherwise cling to it."[27]

The vocabulary of Newspeak was reduced as far as possible, "since the smaller the area of choice, the smaller the temptation to take thought."[28] In the rare instances when feminists have proposed dropping words from common usage, their objective has been to free thought from preconceptions. Eliminating *Mrs.* and *Miss* in favor of *Ms.,* for example, allows the person to be seen as a woman in her own right rather than in relation to someone else. If a dimension that stretches beyond the role of being someone's husband is granted males, women are no less deserving to be seen for themselves. Defending *Ms.* from still another charge of Orwellian manipulation, the poet Ann Sheldon wrote, "What is manipulative is taking the original word 'mistress' and contracting it in two ways, 'Mrs.' and 'Miss,' not for brevity but to indicate whether a woman is a possession or up for grabs. . . . 'Newspeak' of ancient vintage."[29]

A primary requirement of Orwell's invented language was that its words rouse "the minimum of echoes in the speaker's mind."[30] In a magazine article written in 1972 we explored the need to supplement *man* (in its sense of male person) and *woman* with a new term that would avoid the ambiguity of *man* as the slippery equivalent of the human race. The term we proposed was *gen,* as in *genesis* and *generic.* "With such a word," we wrote, "*man* could be used exclusively for males as *woman* is used for females, for *gen* would include both sexes. . . . Like *progenitor, progeny,* and *generation,* it would convey continuity. *Gen* would express the warmth and generalized sexuality of *generous, gentle,* and *genuine;* the specific sexuality of *genital* and *genetic.* In the new family of gen, girls and boys would grow to genhood, and to speak of genkind would be to include all the people of the earth."[31]

To gnash one's teeth over such innovations, as a number of commentators did, is to miss the point. King Canute could not make the waves stand still by commanding them, but as almost every schoolgirl knows, he was not trying to. Feminists realize they cannot expect the language to shed its sexist bias just because they make up new words. Their objective, like King Canute's, is educational. Varda One, editor of *Everywoman,* says that words like *manglish,* as she calls the English language, and *herstory* are "reality-violators and consciousness-raisers." The idea "is to make us realize that language is the basis of our thought and that our thought patterns are steeped in sexism-racism, class snobbery, adult chauvinism, and other louseyvalues."[32] So when women in the movement use *herstory,* their purpose is to emphasize that women's lives, deeds, and participation in human affairs have been neglected or undervalued in standard histories. Similarly, creative female energy is described by Emily Culpepper as *gynergy,* "that impulse in ourselves that has never been possessed by the patriarchy." Ann Sheldon's *phallustine* suggests its own definition, and in Ethel Strainchamps's WASM, the "Protestant" of WASP yields its privilege and influence to "male."[33] Like Loesch's *testeria* and *penisolence,* these neologisms serve a useful function, whether or not they find their way into general use.

What words will eventually replace the outmoded generic unisexisms, no one can predict. Probably most will not be innovations but familiar words recycled. In the stubborn case of the masculine generic pronoun, the candidate that seems most likely to succeed is a word already in wide use, *they.* Despite grammarians' efforts to restrict it to plural antecedents, *they* is already commonly used both in speech and writing as an alternative to the awkward "he or she." What critics of this usage seem not to know, or prefer to ignore, is that *they* and its inflected forms have been used for centuries by reputable writers from Shakespeare ("Everyone to rest themselves") to Shaw ("It's enough to drive anyone out of their senses") to Scott Fitzgerald ("Nobody likes a mind quicker than their own").[34]

Dr. Mary Calderone of the Sex Information and Education Council gave priority to neither sex when she said, "Everybody must develop their own standards of sexual morality,"[35] and the Phone Store doubled its potential market when it advertised, "Give someone a phone of their own." There are precedents for using *they, their,* and *them* not only after *every, each, any, some,* and the like, but after any singular antecedent of indeterminate or inclusive gender. The proper Lord Chesterfield observed in 1759, "If a person is born of a gloomy temper . . . they cannot help it." In our own time those who ignore the stricture of grammarians on this point include President John F. Kennedy ("If that person gets sick . . . they are in the hospital for more than two weeks"); Senator Philip Hart ("I firmly believe that the person who goes for food stamps does it because they are poor"); and Doris Lessing ("And how easy the way a man or woman would come in here, glance around, find smiles and pleasant looks waiting for them, then wave and sit down by themselves").[36]

The use of *they* as a singular pronoun slips out in response to a healthy democratic instinct to include women when general references are made to people. An egalitarian impulse was also involved in the extension of another word—*you*—from the plural to the singular. *Ye* and *you* in Old English were plural pronouns only, the singular forms being *thou* and *thee.* In the late thirteenth century *you* began to be used as the "polite" singular in addressing someone of superior social status or age. Jespersen reports that the habit originated with the Roman emperors, "who desired to be addressed as beings worth more than a single ordinary man," and spread to other European languages in the Middle Ages.[37] The respectful singular *you* soon came to be used by the English gentry when speaking to one another, thus marking a recognition of equality. *Thou* was used, with some inconsistency, both as the form of address for God and between intimates, on the one hand, and for peasants, servants, and children, on the other. In the latter usage, *thou* marked the socially inferior rank of the person spoken to.

When the Quakers, who wished to emphasize the natural equality of all human beings, began to use *thou* and *thee* for everyone, they did not foresee that standard English was moving the other way. In response to the revolutionary spirit of the eighteenth century, the respectful and democratic *you* was extended downward to the masses, and all English-speaking people were able thereafter to address one another as equals. *They* as a singular illustrates once again that in spite of studied efforts to hold it back, our remarkably sensitive tongue is capable of responding to its speakers' longing for equality.

Chapter 9

LANGUAGE AND LIBERATION

When Helen Keller made the connection between the word *water* and the cool substance flowing from a pump across her hand, she ceased to be a little animal, trapped in the prison of a deaf, mute, and sightless body, and became again a being capable of human growth and comprehension. "That living word awakened my soul," she wrote in her autobiography, "gave it light, hope, joy, set it free!"[1]

For the same reasons, language can be described as the oldest human activity: it was the unique adaptation that enabled one group of protohuman animals to release themselves from the blind paths of instinct, of spasmodic attractions and distractions of attention, to think, and so to become more than brute beings. Yet the interdependence of thought and language was barely recognized, much less understood, until a few hundred years ago. And only in the twentieth century, with the convergence of the modern sciences of anthropology and linguistics, has it been possible to demonstrate that we use words not only to communicate our thoughts but to formulate thought as well.

Language enables us to interpret and organize the world we experience through our senses, and in that way it provides structure and meaning to what would otherwise be a jumble of impressions. The corollary, however, is that a language largely limits the thinking of its speakers to ideas they can express in that language. Put another way, language screens reality as a filter on a camera lens screens light waves.

This power of language to shape perception was described by the anthropologist and linguist Edward Sapir in 1928:

> Language is a guide to 'social reality.' . . . [It] powerfully conditions all our thinking about social problems and processes. Human beings do not live in the objective world alone, nor alone in the world of social activity as ordinarily understood, but are very much at the mercy of the particular language which has become the medium of expression for their society. It is quite an illusion to imagine that one adjusts to reality essentially without the use of language and that language is merely an incidental means of solving specific problems of communication or reflection. The fact of the matter is that the 'real world' is to a large extent unconsciously built up on the language habits of the group. . . . We see and hear and otherwise experience very largely as we do because the language habits of our community predispose certain choices of interpretation.[2]

Implementing this theory of linguistic relativity, Sapir's student Benjamin Lee Whorf compared the way languages are constructed in widely divergent cultures. The segmentation of nature, he pointed out, is an aspect of grammar:

> We cut up and organize the spread and flow of events as we do, largely because, through our mother tongue, we are parties to an agreement to do so, not because nature itself is segmented in exactly that way for all to see. Languages differ not only in how they build their sentences but also in how they break down nature to secure the elements to put in those sentences.[3]

Aspects of the hypothesis developed by Sapir and Whorf have been challenged, but the fact that linguistic patterns can direct perception and thinking into certain channels has been demonstrated many times. Furthermore, the lexicon of a given language is responsive to what linguists call the "felt needs" of its speakers.

Since climatic conditions vary widely from one part of the world to another, the terminology used to describe them provides useful illustrations. English, for example, whose native speakers live mainly in the temperate zones, has only one word for snow. The Aztecs, who lived in a tropical and subtropical climate, had a single word to cover snow, ice, and cold.[4] In contrast, Eskimo languages have many different words for snow—snow falling, lying on the ground, drifting, packed for building blocks, and so on—as well as many different words for wind and ice.

The anthropologist Edmund Carpenter, who worked among the Avilik Eskimos, described the ability of Avilik hunters to travel by dogsled across miles of empty, snow-covered tundra. Their awareness of different aspects of snow, ice, wind, and ground contour and the shifting relationships among them—all of which they have words to describe—make it possible for the Avilik to move freely under conditions that would mean certain death to anyone else. Carpenter wrote of the terrain near Hudson Bay where these Eskimo people live:

> There is no line dividing earth from sky. The two are of the same substance. There is no middle distance, no perspec-

> tive, no outline, nothing the eye can cling to except thousands of smokey plumes of snow running along the ground before the wind—a land without bottom or edge. When the wind rises and snow fills the air, visibility may be reduced to a hundred feet or less, and travel becomes dangerous. But, if they must, hunters travel in such weather, even though the trail is lost and the dogs uncertain.
>
> I believe they can do it because of their knowledge of topography and winds. . . . Rarely did a man seem uncertain as to his whereabouts, but as I looked about, at the utter sameness of the earth, I simply could not imagine what reference points he was using.[5]

This ability to perceive minute details and subtle variations in what would to others be a wasteland is essential to the survival of the Avilik, and they have sharpened their perception of these things by embodying them in language. Had they not done so, they would not be able to think as clearly about them or to cope with them as successfully.

Kinship terminology in different languages is of particular interest to anthropologists because it expresses and formalizes relationships that vary from one culture to another. For example, where we have only one word, *uncle,* to stand for one's mother's brother, one's father's brother, or the husband of either parent's sister, some languages have several words for these relationships. In matrilineal societies where a woman's brother has special responsibilities toward her children that her husband's brother does not have, the different words for "uncle" convey entirely different meanings. They are not, in fact, words for "uncle" at all; they signify relationships that do not exist in our culture and for which we therefore need no words.

Relationships do exist in our culture, however, for which words are lacking. In his book *The Liberated Man,* Warren Farrell introduces several terms he feels we should have for a new "human vocabulary": for example, he suggests *attaché* (as in attaché case) for the person with whom one shares one's closest emotional attachment, without reference to sex or kinship; he proposes *living friend* for a person with whom one shares housing for whatever reason (companionship, saving money, security, etc.), whether or not that person is one's attaché.[6] These terms suggest possible solutions to the problem described by Howard Husock in the *Boston Phoenix* when he complained that "we have no single, concise descriptive terms for such a simple concept as that of living on intimate terms with someone—of either sex—without having joined the wedding march." Husock went on:

> You are at a party with your ———, drift off to sample the punch and find yourself involved in conversation. Are you here alone? No, I'm with my . . . friend? Roommate? Good chance that will beg the question. A lover? Perhaps you don't care to discuss your sex life with an imperfect stranger. Nor are sticky situations the only ones where the vacuum is created. An old high school friend calls. How do you describe your current living situation without over- or under-describing? . . .
>
> *Boyfriend/Girlfriend:* When you're 31?
>
> *Person I'm dating:* When you can't even afford dollar night at the Harvard Square Theatre?
>
> *Old man/Old lady:* Common among the hipper-than-thou as well as bikers and dope dealers. Too easily confused with one's parents.
>
> *Fiancé(e):* Common during interviews with landlords, better for obfuscating than clarifying.[7]

In a book called *How to Father,* Fitzhugh Dodson adds a new dimension to a verb that has become depressingly detached in common usage from its noun form.[8] To many speakers of English, perhaps most, the sentence, "He fathered the child" suggests a limited biological act ("She mothered the child," on the other hand, implies a psychological rather than biological relationship), and it may carry the additional inference that after "fathering" the child he had little more to do with it, if indeed he even saw it. One automatically reads Dr. Dodson's title differently. Such manipulation of the language—Dodson also wrote a book called *How to Parent*—may be annoying to some, but there is no denying its effectiveness. "Parenting" cannot be divided into two disparate and mutually exclusive roles, and using the verb "to father" as a parallel of "to mother" invests it with a larger, more intimate, and more human meaning that is immediately recognizable.

We are better at coping with things, whether they involve inanimate nature or human relationships, when we have names for them than when they are nameless or their names are inadequate. But it is only when we become aware that we are struggling to cope with nameless things that we begin to search for words to describe them. This has been illustrated in recent years by the welling up first of black consciousness, then of feminist consciousness. *Racism* was not a word until the 1950s, and it appeared for the first time in an unabridged dictionary when Webster's Third International was published in 1961. A word with similar meaning, *racialism,* had been around for several decades but it was not widely used. In 1901, when the first Webster's International Dictionary came out, English had no single word embodying the idea of prejudice and discrimination based on race. Nor did the language have any term, during most of this century, for prejudice and discrimination based on sex. *Male chauvinism* was first used in the 1960s by women active in civil rights organizations and the Student Left who objected to the demeaning roles to which they were relegated by males in these movements. *Sexism,* probably coined on the analogy of *racism,* entered the language only in the late sixties.

Language expressing the struggle to break with cultural patterns of the past must sometimes precede language expressing newly sensed possibilities for the future. What is happening today with respect to women and words was described in principle by Edward Sapir in 1921:

> The birth of a new concept is invariably foreshadowed by a more or less strained or extended use of old linguistic material; the concept does not attain to individual and independent life until it has found a distinctive linguistic embodiment. . . . As soon as the word is at hand, we instinctively feel, with something of a sigh of relief, that the concept is ours for the handling. Not until we own the symbol do we feel that we hold a key to the immediate knowledge or understanding of the concept.[9]

Even today the sexism deeply ingrained in Western culture is largely nonconscious. As psychologists Sandra and Daryl Bem point out, we can remain unaware of the pervasive ideology that sees females as inferior beings "because alternative beliefs and attitudes about women go unimagined."[10] We have lacked a vocabulary even to formulate such alternatives.

Words that affirm positive qualities in women and girls mainly describe their functions (real or assigned) as females, or like *masculine* in the phrase "She has a masculine mind," or *tomboy,* they take away what they purport to give. "Is there no word for women's *strength*?" asked Sophie Drinker,[11] and what makes her question remarkable is that so few people have thought to ask it.

Among those who did were the editors of the American Heritage School Dictionary. They began their work in 1969 by amassing data for a computerized study of five million words found in a thousand representative books used by children in grades three through nine throughout the United States. The purpose of the study was to help the editors define the words children encounter most frequently in their schoolwork, and to this end the computer produced 700,000 alphabetized citation slips, each showing a word in three lines of context and ranked by the frequency of its occurrence.

What the computer also, and unexpectedly, provided was impeccable evidence that the language of American schoolbooks mirrors the sexist assumptions of society. The schoolbook world, it turned out, was inhabited by twice as many boys as girls and seven times as many men as women. More damaging than this demographic improbability was the social conditioning of young readers through the sex-stereotyped roles and character traits of females and males as the schoolbooks portrayed them. Alma Graham, one of the editors of the school dictionary, wrote: "If this new dictionary were to serve elementary students without showing favoritism to one sex or the other, an effort would have to be made to restore the gender balance. We would need more examples featuring females, and the examples would have to ascribe to girls and women the active, inventive, and adventurous human traits traditionally reserved for men and boys."[12]

Thus the dictionary, published in 1972, became the first in which editors made a conscious effort to correct sexist biases through examples and through the wording of definitions. At the word *daunt,* for instance, the illustration reads, "The difficulty did not daunt her"; at *sole* it is, "She took sole command of the ship." Numerous examples in which *he* is also strong or brave are balanced by others in which the pressure on boys always to be in control of a situation was eased: "His resolve began to waver" and "Tears welled up in his eyes." No doubt most children would like to be indomitable, but girls are not the only ones who waver or whose emotions of gratitude or loss find release in tears. Similarly, in writing definitions the editors consciously dropped some of the sexist assumptions perpetuated by other definers. They defined a *sage,* for example, as "A very wise person, usually old and highly respected," in contrast to the "mature or venerable man sound in judgment" of a widely used college dictionary.

By 1975 many major textbook publishers had adopted or

were preparing to adopt nonsexist guidelines for their authors and editors. The purpose of these guidelines is to give practical examples of how language can be used to liberate and expand thought. Scott, Foresman and Company suggests, for instance, that "When man invented the wheel . . ." can become "When people invented the wheel"; "congressmen" are more inclusively "members of Congress"; and "the typical American . . . he" can be "typical Americans . . . they." A sentence like, "In New England, the typical farm was so small that the owner and his sons could take care of it by themselves," can more accurately be phrased, "In New England, the typical farm was so small that the family members could take care of it by themselves."[13] Amplifying this kind of distinction in more comprehensive guidelines based on an analysis of social studies textbooks, Elizabeth Burr, Susan Dunn, and Norma Farquhar wrote, "phrases such as 'the farmer's wife' clearly convey the idea that the female was merely a possession of the farmer and was not herself a farmer, when in fact the wives of most small farmers were themselves farmers *in every sense of the word.*"[14]

McGraw-Hill's guidelines received unusually extensive publicity and were widely distributed. Requests for the document came from government agencies, corporations, communications media, religious organizations, schools and universities, as well as thousands of individuals. One author who writes on business management and who had always assumed that his readership was overwhelmingly male, reported doing a turnabout after reading the guidelines. "I've been talking to a lot of business women," he said, "and find they *would* like to find books that included them and did not pretend they never existed in the business world. . . . There are 35 million women in the U.S. work force today."[15]

Some authors whose subjects have traditionally been considered male domains did not need guidelines to tell them that women resent being excluded. Some years ago a woman who had bought an old farmhouse in Maine and was remodeling it on her own wrote to Hubbard H. Cobb, author of *How to Buy and Remodel the Older House:* "My heartfelt thanks for using the words 'people' and 'a man or woman' in reference to homebuyers, builders, architects, etc. I've acquired a small library of how-to books ranging from masonry to heating, and the authors invariably use only the word 'man.' It's strange to admit but they make me feel so left out, especially when they add in passing that 'the little woman' might like such and such a style! . . . After all, I paid for the place myself, and I'm doing a large part of the work myself."[16]

Library cataloguers are carrying out a widespread campaign to revise the traditional use of subsuming and sexist language in subject headings and card catalogue descriptions as well as in the terminology of cataloguing instructions. "Women, children, the mentally and physically handicapped, and racial, sexual, and other minorities . . . fall outside the assumed norm and therefore qualify for separate and unequal categorization," Elizabeth Dickinson wrote in 1974 of the Library of Congress subject headings used in libraries throughout the country.[17] Dickinson is a cataloguer at the Hennepin County Library in Minnesota where a group under the leadership of Sanford Berman, head cataloguer, is coordinating nationwide efforts to bring pressure for reform on the Library of Congress and the American Library Association. As part of this effort, Joan K. Marshall, the chief cataloguer at the Brooklyn College Library, prepared a position paper in which she makes the point that "language, if permitted to change only at its own pace and that of the mass mind, is conservative if not reactionary." But, Marshall goes on, "Women have decided, quite simply, that that pace is not fast enough. We know that any genuine change in our status in society is inextricably tied to change in our language. And with that knowledge comes the conviction that we can increase the rate of change."[18]

The council of the American Library Association acknowledged in 1975 that many of its official documents and publications "use nouns and pronouns with strictly male connotations" and further that "consistent and exclusive use of the masculine gender perpetuates the traditional language of society which discriminates against women." The council therefore resolved: "That future publications and official documents of the American Library Association avoid terminology which perpetuates sex stereotypes, and existing publications and official documents, as they are revised, be changed to avoid such terminology."[19]

Another gain in eliminating separate and unequal categorization was made when the United States Department of Labor revised its list of occupational classifications to drop sex-stereotyped job titles. For the most part the changes were accomplished by replacing the suffix *-man* with common gender terms such as *operator* or *worker.* Carmen R. Maymi, director of the Women's Bureau of the department, called the new job titles a welcome step toward ending sex discrimination in employment. "It is not realistic to expect that women will apply for job openings advertised for foremen, salesmen or credit men," she said. "Nor will men apply for job vacancies calling for laundresses, maids, or airline stewardesses."[20] On the same grounds, Mary M. Fuller, a management education specialist who advises government and private organizations, points out that the generic *he* covertly promotes economic discrimination and is inappropriate for use in job descriptions. In a position paper published in the *Training and Development Journal* she wrote, "Categorizing . . . by characteristics other than the ability to get the job done is now illegal as well as economically foolish for the total society."[21]

Legislation enforcing equal job opportunities has helped to expose and eradicate employment terminology prejudicial to women. In one case a federal court found a major airline guilty of discrimination against its female flight attendants: by calling women "stewardesses" and calling men performing the identical job "pursers," the company had camouflaged widely unequal pay and promotion schedules.[22]

The response of different religious bodies to linguistic

change has varied widely, as might be expected. Whether ignored or acknowledged, however, the issue has theological implications. In fundamentalist sects like the one led by the Reverend Bill Gothard, which teach that in families a chain of command exists from God to the husband to the wife to the children,[23] male domination in language is presumably accepted as divinely ordained. Other religious groups recognize the linguistic exclusion of females as a scandal that must be resolved, and many have gone beyond mere lip service. In the vanguard was the United Church of Christ, which by action of its General Synod in 1973 committed itself "to the elimination of sex and race discrimination in every area of its life." To implement that affirmation the constitution and by-laws of the United Church, as well as all its printed materials, including worship books and services, hymnals, curricula, journals, magazines, and personnel documents are being written or revised "to make all language deliberately inclusive."[24]

Gates of Prayer, a revision of the Union Prayerbook published in 1975 by the Central Conference of American Rabbis, contains a number of references to the great women of Hebrew history, including "God of our mothers, God of Sarah, Rebekah, Leah, and Rachel, Deborah, Hannah, and Ruth" as a parallel to "God of our fathers, God of Abraham, Isaac, and Jacob, Amos, Isaiah, and Micah." Elsewhere Rachel and Leah are identified as "the Mothers of this people Israel" and the phrase "God of all generations" has been substituted for "God of our fathers." In their introduction the editors noted that "while our themes are the ageless ones of our tradition, the manner of their expression reflects our own day. . . . Our commitment in the Reform movement to the equality of the sexes is of long standing. In this book, it takes the form of avoiding the use of masculine terminology exclusively, when we are referring to the human race in general."[25]

The implications of these and similar revisions[26] were spelled out at some length in guidelines published in 1974 by the editors of the interfaith publication, the *Journal of Ecumenical Studies:*

> From the time of the Genesis story, human beings have been aware of the power involved in being able to name something or someone. If anything, men and women have become even more aware of the importance of language in the creation of their world, externally as well as internally, with the advent of modern linguistic analysis. Every significant human movement, social, political, economic—and religious—develops its own special language which helps form its adherents and project an influential image of itself to outsiders. . . .
>
> One of the most significant human movements of our day is feminism, i.e., the movement to acquire justice for women equally with men. One result of this movement is a growing awareness of sexism in our language, which most often takes the form of assuming that the male is the true human ideal. Such male dominance in language can be called linguistic sexism.[27]

Specifically, the editors of the journal asked that anyone submitting material to them for publication avoid, except in direct quotations or for other special reasons, all sex-based generic terminology, including references to God by masculine pronouns and the use of feminine pronouns "to refer to entities such as the Church or Israel." Of the latter they said:

> Such usage normally reflects the assumption that the feminine is inferior to the masculine, as with the feminine Church, or Israel, vis-à-vis a masculine God. It is clear that Israel, the Church, etc., are subordinate to God. But, upon reflection, it should also be clear that the feminine-masculine imagery used in the Jewish, Christian, Muslim, and other traditions is an attempt to express that inferior-supe-

rior, human-divine relationship in language that reflected the then (and often, still) existing inferior-superior, female-male societal relationship. But once the position that "all humans are created equal" is accepted, such language is no longer acceptable.[28]

Religious and secular guidelines are often greeted with dismay by alarmists who jump to the conclusion that the Bible or the classics are going to be rewritten along the lines George Orwell suggested in *Nineteen Eighty-Four.* No such suggestion has ever been made, except in ridicule, but the question remains, if *man* becomes an unequivocal symbol for the human male—the complement and companion of *woman*—how will future generations understand the writings of past authors who intended (or thought they intended) to include both sexes when they used the word? What will readers in the twenty-first century make of the question phrased in sixteenth-century English, "What is man that thou art mindful of him?"

What do we make of it now? Is not the man of whom the psalmist writes the same man to whom Moses delivered the commandment "Thou shalt not covet thy neighbor's wife"? Our descendants will know, just as we know, that our tongue has for centuries mirrored the myth of the male as the true human ideal, and much of what was written in the screened light of that myth will remain part of their heritage. But our greatest literature is not bound by half-visioned myths, and it will survive the semantic narrowing of masculine terms just as it has survived semantic changes in the past.

When Chaucer wrote of one of the Canterbury pilgrims, "He was a gentle harlot and a kind, a better fellow should men not find," he was not calling that gentle pilgrim a whore. In the fourteenth century, *harlot* simply meant "good fellow."[29] In Shakespeare's time *child* was ambiguous in much the same way *man* has become: a child was a young person of either sex, but especially a female. *Bearn,* the Old English word for "son," had become *barne* and widened its meaning to "child" in the sense we use the word *child* today. So in *The Winter's Tale* a shepherd who finds an abandoned baby says, "What have we here? Mercy on 's, a barne; a very pretty barne! A boy or a child, I wonder?"[30] The word *girl* used to mean a young person of either sex, but by the sixteen hundreds it had begun to be narrowed and was in the process of replacing the special feminine-gender meaning of *child*. Eventually, of course, *child* replaced *barne* and *girl* was restricted to young females. Just as glossaries are helpful to a twentieth-century reader of Chaucer and Shakespeare, so they can be expected to help readers of a future age interpret words whose meanings have changed in the inevitable process of continuing linguistic evolution.

Sometimes the process of change involves a return to earlier uses. *Fellow*, for example, is an ancient word with a history of varied and conflicting meanings, but it is being used today with much of its Old English meaning intact: "One who shares with another in a possession, official dignity, or in the performance of any work; a partner, colleague, co-worker. Also one united with another in a covenant for common ends; an ally." The Oxford English Dictionary, noting that this earliest meaning is obsolete, goes on to give twelve other definitions of the noun, including a spouse of either sex (Shakespeare used it to mean "wife" in *The Tempest*), a servant, one of the common people, and a person who holds an academic award or membership in a learned society.[31] Yet we still recognize the Old English sense when we speak of fellowship or use a combination term like *fellow student*. Although *fellow* alone is applied colloquially more often to a boy or man than to a girl or woman, one can also say without constraint, "She's a good fellow," as one cannot say, "She's a good man."

The most far-reaching revolutions have been inspired by nothing more (or less) than seeing the obvious from a new perspective. The knowledge that the earth is not the center of the universe seemed at first to shatter the collective ego of the Western world. The recognition that "man" is not the species is also revolutionary, and in its way equally frightening. For as in the Copernican Revolution, the challenge is to an article of faith, an accepted dogma sanctified by Church and State, protected by tradition, and embedded in language.

Until 1543 when the Copernican theory was published, the word *revolution* referred primarily to the motion of a body in orbit; after that time it also came to mean, especially in the adjective *revolutionary,* a fundamental change in thought or organization. The revolution we are living through challenges the dominance of patriarchal structures.

In a time of change it is not enough to hang on to the old ways of seeing the universe or society. Not to look ahead is to be left behind. Michael Korda, author of *Male Chauvinism!,* puts it this way: "Women are thinking out their roles; men are merely clinging desperately to theirs, hoping that they will survive the coming storm, searching for the means to prevent its happening."[32] Perhaps the distinction is overstated, but it touches on the real pain involved in efforts to imagine the new options we need to pursue if our perverse journey toward destruction is to be altered. It is time we looked more carefully at where the thoughtless use of sexual stereotypes is taking us. Man as leader, woman as follower; man as producer, woman as consumer; man as strength, woman as weakness—this is the cosmography that has brought us to man as aggressor, humanity as victim.

In a discussion of the loss that can result when an activity is artificially limited to one sex, Margaret Mead once used this example:

> There are societies that wished to achieve the full beauty of a chorus which spanned the possibilities of the human voice, but in linking religion and music together also wished to ban women, as unsuited for an active rôle in the church, from the choir. Boys' voices provide an apparently good substitute. So also do eunuchs, and so in the end we

> may have music modelled on a perfect orchestration of men's and women's voices, but at the price of the exclusion of women and the castration of men.[33]

It is an apt example.

Exclusion is another form of castration. For *castration,* in addition to its literal meaning—to remove the gonads of either sex—also means a depriving of vigor. One dictionary defines "castration complex" as "the often unconscious fear or feeling of bodily injury or loss of power at the hands of authority."[34] Why, then, is castration more often associated with male loss of power than female? Why do we not refer to "castrating males" in connection with the losses women have suffered under a system that renders them impotent? Can it be because Authority is male? Because the Establishment is male? To admit women to full human membership is a threat to male prerogatives, and women who challenge this "natural" order are called "castrating women." We forget, or refuse to acknowledge, the reality that men are more often the castraters of each other and of women. Used carelessly, the word assumes the warp our culture imposes, just as, used carelessly, language castrates thought.

Sexist expressions like "castrating women," "the man in the street," "bitch goddess Success," and "the weaker sex" are ready made. Ready-made phrases, as George Orwell said in his essay "Politics and the English Language," are the prefabricated strips of words and mixed metaphors that come crowding in when you do not want to take the trouble to think through what you are saying. "They will construct your sentences for you," he said, "—even think your thoughts for you, to a certain extent—and at need they will perform the important service of partially concealing your meaning even from yourself."[35]

To whom does one refer these days when invoking "the man in the street"? Why does the metaphor "bitch goddess" hang on? The Reverend Harvey Cox may have provided a clue to that when he came up with these images of female sexuality in an article on women priests. "What the conservatives fear, I welcome: a Christian sacrament enriched by the presence at the altar of the Great Mother, the Scarlet Woman, the Whore of Babylon and the Virgin Queen." Counterparts, perhaps, of the Great White Father, Jack the Ripper, Casanova, and King Henry the Eighth? What else can one conclude, since the point Cox was making was that women should become priests "not because they are no different from men, but because they are different."[36]

And what, exactly, does *weaker* mean in "the weaker sex"? Or *fair*? Is that still a reference to beauty? Or complexion? Or does it now refer to fairness in sports or politics or everyday dealings in the shop, office, or home?

"The whole tendency of modern prose is away from concreteness," Orwell lamented. He urged the "scrapping of every word or idiom that has outgrown its usefulness. . . . What is above all needed is to let the meaning choose the word, and not the other way about. In prose, the worst thing one can do with words is surrender to them."[37]

When sexist language is deliberate, writers and speakers have a rich store of words to choose from. More often sexist language is not deliberate: it is either subconscious or lazy. It is easier to talk about all doctors and hospital patients as *he* and all nurses as *she.* Much easier to accept the masculine/feminine stereotypes than to think them through in relation to real people. Simpler by far to speak of the next President of the United States or the next chancellor of the university or the next head of the local school board as though, inevitably, they will be male.

Eliminating sexism need not result in graceless language, as many people fear. Sensitive speakers, writers, and editors have been doing it consciously and well for years. Language that does not depend on abstraction is superior, for it is forced to be specific. The number of people who are refusing to surrender to linguistic sexism is relatively small, but it will grow. When that happens, the faults of those less sensitive will become even more apparent.

Our vocabulary is already being affected by the increasing equality of women and men under the law. As women continue to gain recognition in commerce, government, the professions, the arts, and higher education, the process will be accelerated. Most important, children acquiring language in their formative years will be free to imagine and explore the full range of their human potential. Significant gains have been made in many areas, but the transformation of English in response to the movement for human liberation has scarcely begun.

Postscript

Let the Meaning Choose the Word

The "rules" that govern the "correct" use of a language have much in common with other social rules. They are not immutable, ordained to last forever; they evolved to meet social needs, and they are sensitive to social change. Some serve a useful purpose. Others are oppressive or have become outmoded: they are, in Shakespeare's phrase, "more honored in the breach than the observance."

The question is, how do you know when to abandon a word or phrase or grammatical rule that is still cited by language authorities as correct? We think the answer depends on a simple test: does the term or usage contribute to clarity and accuracy, or does it fudge them?

When you are faced with a particular problem of usage, this approach also helps to produce an alternative that avoids the original difficulty. For example, if it is your understanding that male human beings were solely responsible for the domestication of animals, then a sentence beginning "When man first domesticated animals . . ." conveys your meaning (even if its accuracy is highly suspect). If the possibility exists that women played some part in the process, however, then in the English we speak today the phrase "When man first domesticated animals" conveys misinformation. "When human beings first domesticated animals" or "our ancestors" or "early people" does a more accurate job.

A problem of incongruity may remain. At what point do you make the transition from an outmoded old usage to an awkward-sounding new one? The kind of person who tries to be open to change has an easier time moving with linguistic evolution than those who habitually react to change as unpleasant or frightening. But even the latter have given up whalebone corsets and starched wing collars without assuming they have to switch to miniskirts or tank tops. To address someone's great-grandmother as Ms. could be insensitive, but to speak of her only in terms of her late husband's life and achievements is rather like saying that she should always wear widow's weeds.

We have not attempted in what follows to present a comprehensive set of guidelines. We have tried, instead, to isolate the chief areas where unconscious, sexist assumptions get in the way of accurate and felicitous writing and speech. Most of the sexist offenses committed through language are not deliberate. They creep in as a result of laziness, habit, or overreliance on what the rule books say is correct, and they yield to the test of exactness. Although some solutions cannot be applied across the board, since their appropriateness varies with the circumstances, most involve nothing more than a healthy respect for fairness and precision. What's sauce for the goose is sauce for the gander, and the other way about.

Animals

Animals, with the exception of some of the lower forms, are either female or male. This is true of the rabbit devastating the lettuce crop, the turtle crossing the road, the cockroach scuttling under the baseboard, the osprey riding an updraft. Yet many people, including some who pride themselves on their knowledge of natural history, habitually refer to the rabbit, the turtle, the cockroach, and the osprey as "he." Why, is a mystery, especially since the pronoun *it* provides an acceptable way, when the sex of a particular animal is not known, to avoid a 50 percent chance of error. Evidence is mounting that children are confused by this use of *he,* and that the grammatical convention condoning it is one source of a prevalent subconscious assumption that maleness is the norm.

Babies (and by Extension Muslims, Medical Students, Americans, Politicians, et al.)

All babies are not alike, and all babies are not male, despite the impression many baby-care books give to the contrary. What makes authors who write about babies especially prone to using the masculine generic pronoun is that all mothers, unlike their offspring, really are female, and referring to a mother as "she" leaves *he* as the handiest tag for a child. One solution, when talking or writing about babies in general, is to use the plural, especially since "most babies," "some babies," "babies are usually . . ." have the advantage of being more accurate than sweeping generalizations about "the baby." When it is desirable to generalize in the singular, it is usually possible to keep a particular baby in mind, perhaps even to give it a name. Since particular babies are either female or male, they obligingly provide their own sets of pronouns. Eliminating the generic *he* avoids the suggestion that males are more important or more typical than females, and it also frees the parents of a girl-baby from having to figure out whether in a given instance the author is talking about boys only or both boys and girls.

The temptation to use *he* when generalizing about the people babies grow into can also lead to oversimplification. Again, avoiding sentences that refer to them with singular third-person pronouns is one way to reflect demographic realities.

-Ess Endings

Since authors, poets, sculptors, and actors may be either female or male, the significance of a word like *authoress* is not that it identifies a female but that it indicates deviation from what is consciously or unconsciously considered the standard. Tacking an *-ess* ending onto a common gender English word because the person referred to is a woman is reasonably resented by most people so identified. When it is relevant to make a special point of someone's sex, pronouns are useful and so are the adjectives *male* and *female.*

-Ette Endings

The suffix *-ette* indicates feminine gender in French words and frequently has nothing to do with sex, as in *bicyclette,* which means "bicycle." In English the suffix has three functions: to indicate imitation, as in *flannelette;* to denote small size, as in *dinette;* and to suggest that females need not be taken seriously, as in *farmerette* and *astronette.* By implication an usherette is a frivolous little woman hired to replace a bona fide usher.

Feminine and *Masculine*

Except in grammar and rhyme, the terms *feminine* and *masculine* and their noun forms, *femininity* and *masculinity,* are so protean that they always warrant careful examination. They do not refer to femaleness and maleness but to arbitrary categories of appearance, personality, behavior, and activity that a given society or individual holds to be suitable. Since what is considered "masculine" or "feminine" will be different tomorrow from what it was yesterday, using either word carelessly may reinforce arbitrary double standards that suppress spontaneity and individuality in people of both sexes.

Forms of Address

The purpose of a social title (or courtesy title, or honorific) is to indicate respect for the person addressed. Ironically, one often conveys more respect for a woman by avoiding the conventional courtesy titles than by using them, since the distinction they make is related to a woman's marital state rather than to the person herself. In addition, the term chosen may be based on an erroneous assumption. Therefore, unless a woman's preference in titles is known, courtesy and honor may be better served by addressing her, in either speech or writing, by her first and last names together.

One reason people are uneasy about using *Ms.*, an obvious solution to the Miss/Mrs. dilemma, is that it is still so new it makes them self-conscious, with the result that they end up emphasizing the title rather than the name: "Good morning, *Mr.* Smithers," sounds sarcastic, and so does "Good morning, *Ms.* Smithers." As the title becomes more widely used the difficulty will disappear.

He as a Common Gender Pronoun

The use of masculine pronouns to include female referents, as in "the average reader . . . he," is part of the linguistic male-as-norm syndrome. Since English lacks a truly generic third-person-singular pronoun, those who want to avoid both exclusiveness and ambiguity sometimes feel obliged to use "he or she" and sometimes "she or he." This device works unless the phrase must be repeated frequently, in which case it can become ludicrous. Another approach is to recast the sentence to omit third-person pronouns entirely: "If a student is unable to complete the course, he may apply for a refund" can be said more succinctly, "A student who is unable to complete the course may apply for a refund." Or the sentence can be phrased in the plural. "The visitor is invited to familiarize himself with the map before entering the park" is less cold when cast in the plural, and more to the point—unless, of course, the park is reserved for men and boys.

Job Titles

When a job is open to members of both sexes, describing it by a common gender term is more accurate and more conducive to effective recruiting than using one title for men and another for women. The same is true for elective offices that acquired male designations because—like congressman, alderman, and vestryman—they were held only by men in the past. Ever since Jeannette Rankin broke the congressional sex barrier in 1917, referring to "members of Congress," "the men and women in Congress," or "U.S. representatives" has been more exact than using "congressmen" as a collective. Once an individual assumes an office or job, titles like *congresswoman* or *congressman, newspaperwoman* or *newspaperman, forewoman* or *foreman* are obvious choices.

Male as Norm

Who knows when a reference to "our forefathers" is intended to include "our foremothers" or when an evocation of "brotherhood" is meant to exclude the ladies' auxiliary? Words like *forebears* and *ancestors* are more accurate when inclusiveness is the aim, and a phrase that brings to mind the humanity common to both sexes leaves the words *brotherhood* and *sisterhood* to describe the special bonds that members of each sex feel for one another.

Man as the Species

The use of *man* to represent the human species reinforces the erroneous notion that the species is male or at least that the male is more representative than the female. A sentence like "Man is a tool-using animal" is misleading, since women also use tools. "Human beings are tool-using animals" says what it means. "Man is slowly destroying himself by polluting his environment" is doubly fuzzy. Even if one argues that most of the people responsible for industrial pollution are men, the results affect the health of females as well as males. "Humans are slowly destroying themselves by polluting their environment" gets around both faults and suggests that everyone will have to become involved in solving the problem.

Man as Typical

"The man who pays taxes," "the working man," "one man, one vote," all imply that the typical person who pays taxes, works, or votes is male. "Taxpayers," "workers" or "working people," "one person, one vote," do not. "Men of good will" number approximately half of all people of good will, give or take a few thousand.

Order

In word pairs like *male and female, men and women, husbands and wives, sons and daughters, boys and girls, Adam and Eve,* males need not always come first. Occasionally reversing the order has two advantages: it counters the implication that members of the male sex rate a priority, and it helps to jog attention by avoiding the habitual. "Ladies and gentlemen" is a polite but empty form of address people use when talking to a group that includes women and men. Once the amenities have been taken care of and the speaker gets down to matters of substance, however, women are again relegated to second place or lose out altogether to broad-stroke generalizations about "man." Specifically including women and making a conscious effort to avoid the hackneyed order can have the effect of bringing real people to mind instead of clichés.

-Person Compounds

Salesperson is a word that doesn't seem to throw anyone into a tizzy. This acceptance probably came about because *salesman* and *saleswoman* had already been used for many years as parallel sex-designating terms by the time the need was felt for a common gender term that could refer to either. As more women serve in posts once exclusively held by males, *-person* compounds will come to seem more natural. They are especially useful when candidates for a job or elective office are being considered without regard to sex.

Plural Constructions

Plural constructions help to avoid the built-in male-as-norm quality English has acquired, and they also provide a useful way to escape the trap of generalizing in the singular. "The Indian . . . he" omits half the Indian population. It implies in addition that all Indians can be described in terms of one Indian. Plurals do not automatically solve either problem, but they invite a certain amount of healthy qualification that the singular construction does not.

They as a Singular Pronoun

For more than four hundred years, reputable writers and speakers of English have used *they, their, them,* and *themselves* as singular pronouns for indefinite antecedents.

The Term *Womanly*

This word is not parallel to *manly* because instead of describing human attributes, as *manly* does, it is limited to qualities assumed to be appropriate to or characteristic of females—and inappropriate to or uncharacteristic of males. A woman who is courageous, strong, and resolute cannot be called either manly or womanly. The only solution at present seems to be to call her courageous, strong, and resolute.

Appendix

ONE SMALL STEP FOR GENKIND

Casey Miller and Kate Swift

First published in *The New York Times Magazine* of April 16, 1972, this article has been reprinted in numerous textbooks and college readers. It is included here because it was one of the earliest articles to attract widespread attention to the sexist nature of standard English, and because the interest it evoked provided the incentive for this book.

A riddle is making the rounds that goes like this: A man and his young son were in an automobile accident. The father was killed and the son, who was critically injured, was rushed to a hospital. As attendants wheeled the unconscious boy into the emergency room, the doctor on duty looked down at him and said, "My God, it's my son!" What was the relationship of the doctor to the injured boy?

If the answer doesn't jump to your mind, another riddle

that has been around a lot longer might help: The blind beggar had a brother. The blind beggar's brother died. The brother who died had no brother. What relation was the blind beggar to the blind beggar's brother?

As with all riddles, the answers are obvious once you see them: the doctor was the boy's mother and the beggar was her brother's sister. Then why doesn't everyone solve them immediately? Mainly because our language, like the culture it reflects, is male oriented. To say that a woman in medicine is an exception is simply to confirm that statement. Thousands of doctors are women, but in order to be seen in the mind's eye, they must be called "women doctors."

Except for words that refer to females by definition (*mother, actress, congresswoman*), and words for occupations traditionally held by females (*nurse, secretary, prostitute*), the English language defines everyone as male. The hypothetical person ("If a man can walk ten miles in two hours . . ."), the average person ("the man in the street"), and the active person ("the man on the move") are male. The assumption is that unless otherwise identified, people in general—including doctors and beggars—are men. It is a semantic mechanism that operates to keep women invisible: *man* and *mankind* represent everyone; *he* in generalized use refers to either sex; the "land where our fathers died" is also the land of our mothers—although they go unsung. As the beetle-browed and mustachioed man in a Steig cartoon says to his two male drinking companions, "When I speak of mankind, one thing I *don't* mean is womankind."

Semantically speaking, woman is not one with the species of man, but a distinct subspecies. "Man," says the 1971 edition of the Britannica Junior Encyclopædia, "is the highest form of life on earth. His superior intelligence, combined with certain physical characteristics, have enabled man to achieve things that are impossible for other animals." (The prose style has something in common with the report of a research team describing its studies on "the development of the uterus in rats, guinea pigs and men.") As though quoting the Steig character, still speaking to his friends in McSorley's, the Junior Encyclopædia continues: "Man must invent most of his behavior, because he lacks the instincts of lower animals. . . . Most of the things he learns have been handed down from his ancestors by language and symbols rather than by biological inheritance."

Considering that for the last 5,000 years society has been patriarchal, that statement explains a lot. It explains why Eve was made from Adam's rib instead of the other way around, and who invented all those Adam-rib words like *fe*male and *wo*man in the first place. It also explains why, when it is necessary to mention woman, the language makes her a lower caste, a class separate from the rest of man; why it works to "keep her in her place."

This inheritance through language and other symbols begins in the home (also called a man's castle) where man and wife (not husband and wife, or man and woman) live for a while with their children. It is reinforced by religious training, the educational system, the press, government, commerce, and the law. As Andrew Greeley wrote not long ago in this magazine, "Man is a symbol-creating animal. He orders and interprets his reality by his symbols, and he uses the symbols to reconstruct that reality."

Consider some of the reconstructed realities of American history. When schoolchildren learn from their textbooks that the early colonists gained valuable experience in governing themselves, they are not told that the early colonists who were women were denied the privilege of self-government; when they learn that in the eighteenth century the average man had to manufacture many of the things he and his family needed, they are not told that this "average man" was often a woman who manufactured much of what she and her family needed. Young people learn that intrepid pioneers crossed the country in covered wagons with their wives, children, and cattle; they do not learn that women themselves were intrepid pioneers rather than part of the baggage.

In a paper published this year in Los Angeles as a guide for authors and editors of social-studies textbooks, Elizabeth Burr, Susan Dunn, and Norma Farquhar document unintentional skewings of this kind that occur either because women are not specifically mentioned as affecting or being affected by historical events, or because they are discussed in terms of outdated assumptions. "One never sees a picture of women captioned simply 'farmers' or 'pioneers,' " they point out. The subspecies nomenclature that requires a caption to read "women farmers" or "women pioneers" is extended to impose certain jobs on women by definition. The textbook guide gives as an example the word *housewife,* which it says not only "suggests that domestic chores are the exclusive burden of females," but gives "female students the idea that they were born to keep house and teaches male students that they are automatically entitled to laundry, cooking and housecleaning services from the women in their families."

Sexist language is any language that expresses such stereotyped attitudes and expectations, or that assumes the inherent superiority of one sex over the other. When a woman says of her husband, who has drawn up plans for a new bedroom wing and left out closets, "Just like a man," her language is as sexist as the man's who says, after his wife has changed her mind about needing the new wing after all, "Just like a woman."

Male and *female* are not sexist words, but *masculine* and *feminine* almost always are. *Male* and *female* can be applied objectively to individual people and animals and, by extension, to things. When electricians and plumbers talk about male and female couplings, everyone knows or can figure out what they mean. The terms are graphic and culture-free.

Masculine and *feminine,* however, are as sexist as any

words can be, since it is almost impossible to use them without invoking cultural stereotypes. When people construct lists of "masculine" and "feminine" traits they almost always end up making assumptions that have nothing to do with innate differences between the sexes. We have a friend who happens to be going through the process of pinning down this very phenomenon. He is seven years old and his question concerns why his coats and shirts button left over right while his sister's button the other way. He assumes it must have something to do with the differences between boys and girls, but he can't see how.

What our friend has yet to grasp is that the way you button your coat, like most sex-differentiated customs, has nothing to do with real differences but much to do with what society wants you to feel about yourself as a male or female person. Society decrees that it is appropriate for girls to dress differently from boys, to act differently, and to think differently. Boys must be masculine, whatever that means, and girls must be feminine.

Unabridged dictionaries are a good source for finding out what society decrees to be appropriate, though less by definition than by their choice of associations and illustrations. Words associated with males—*manly, virile,* and *masculine,* for example—are defined through a broad range of positive attributes like strength, courage, directness, and independence, and they are illustrated through such examples of contemporary usage as "a manly determination to face what comes," "a virile literary style," "a masculine love of sports." Corresponding words associated with females are defined with fewer attributes (though weakness is often one of them) and the examples given are generally negative if not clearly pejorative: "feminine wiles," "womanish tears," "a womanlike lack of promptness," "convinced that drawing was a waste of time, if not downright womanly."

Male-associated words are frequently applied to females

to describe something that is either incongruous ("a mannish voice") or presumably commendable ("a masculine mind," "she took it like a man"), but female-associated words are unreservedly derogatory when applied to males, and are sometimes abusive to females as well. The opposite of *masculine* is *effeminate,* although the opposite of *feminine* is simply *unfeminine.*

One dictionary, after defining the word *womanish* as "suitable to or resembling a woman," further defines it as "unsuitable to a man or to a strong character of either sex." Words derived from *sister* and *brother* provide another apt example, for whereas *sissy,* applied either to a male or female, conveys the message that sisters are expected to be timid and cowardly, *buddy* makes clear that brothers are friends.

The subtle disparagement of females and corresponding approbation of males wrapped up in many English words is painfully illustrated by *tomboy.* Here is an instance where a girl who likes sports and the out-of-doors, who is curious about how things work, who is adventurous and bold instead of passive, is defined in terms of something she is not—a boy. By denying that she can be the person she is and still be a girl, the word surreptitiously undermines her sense of identity; it says she is unnatural. A "tomboy," as defined by one dictionary, is a "girl, especially a young girl, who behaves like a spirited boy." But who makes the judgment that she is acting like a spirited boy, not a spirited girl? Can it be a coincidence that in the case of the dictionary just quoted the editor, executive editor, managing editor, general manager, all six members of the Board of Linguists, the usage editor, science editor, all six general editors of definitions, and 94 out of the 104 distinguished experts consulted on usage—are men?

It isn't enough to say that any invidious comparisons and stereotypes lexicographers perpetuate are already present in the culture. There are ways to define words like *womanly* and *tomboy* that don't put women down, though the tradition has been otherwise. Samuel Johnson, the lexicographer, was the same Dr. Johnson who said, "A woman preaching is like a dog's walking on his hind legs. It is not done well; but you are surprised to find it done at all."

Possibly because of the negative images associated with *womanish* and *womanlike,* and with expressions like "woman driver" and "woman of the street," the word *woman* dropped out of fashion for a time. The women at the office and the women on the assembly line and the women one first knew in school all became ladies or girls or gals. Now a countermovement, supported by the very term *women's liberation,* is putting back into words like *woman* and *sister* and *sisterhood* the meaning they were losing by default. It is as though, in the nick of time, women had seen that the language itself could destroy them.

Some long-standing conventions of the news media add insult to injury. When a woman or girl makes news, her sex is identified at the beginning of a story, if possible in the headline or its equivalent. The assumption, apparently, is that whatever event or action is being reported, a woman's involvement is less common and therefore more newsworthy than a man's. If the story is about achievement, the implication is: "pretty good for a woman." And because people are assumed to be male unless otherwise identified, the media have developed a special and extensive vocabulary to avoid the constant repetition of *woman.* The results—"Grandmother Wins Nobel Prize," "Blonde Hijacks Airliner," "Housewife to Run for Congress"—convey the kind of information that would be ludicrous in comparable headlines if the subjects were men. Why, if "Unsalaried Husband to Run for Congress" is unacceptable to editors, do women have to keep explaining that to describe them through external or superficial concerns reflects a sexist view of women as decorative objects, breeding machines, and extensions of men, not real people?

Members of the Chicago chapter of the National Organization for Women recently studied the newspapers in their area and drew up a set of guidelines for the press. These include cutting out descriptions of the "clothes, physical features, dating life and marital status of women where such references would be considered inappropriate if about men"; using language in such a way as to include women in copy that refers to homeowners, scientists, and business people where "newspaper descriptions often convey the idea that all such persons are male"; and displaying the same discretion in printing generalizations about women as would be shown toward racial, religious, and ethnic groups. "Our concern with what we are called may seem trivial to some people," the women said, "but we regard the old usages as symbolic of women's position within this society."

The assumption that an adult woman is flattered by being called a girl is matched by the notion that a woman in a menial or poorly paid job finds compensation in being called a lady. Ethel Strainchamps has pointed out that since *lady* is used as an adjective with nouns designating both high and low occupations (lady wrestler, lady barber, lady doctor, lady judge), some writers assume they can use the noun form without betraying value judgments. Not so, Strainchamp says, rolling the issue into a spitball: "You may write, 'He addressed the Republican ladies,' or 'The Democratic ladies convened' . . . but I have never seen 'the Communist ladies' or 'the Black Panther ladies' in print."

Thoughtful writers and editors have begun to repudiate some of the old usages. *Divorcée, grandmother,* and *blonde,* along with *vivacious, pert, dimpled,* and *cute,* were dumped by the *Washington Post* in the spring of 1970 by the executive editor, Benjamin Bradlee. In a memo to his staff, Bradlee wrote, "The meaningful equality and dignity of women is properly under scrutiny today . . . because this equality has been less than meaningful and the dignity not always free of stereotype and condescension."

What women have been called in the press—or at least the part that operates above ground—is only a fraction of the infinite variety of alternatives to *woman* used in the subcultures of the English-speaking world. Beyond "chicks," "dolls," "dames," "babes," "skirts," and "broads" are the words and phrases in which women are reduced to their sexuality and nothing more. It would be hard to think of another area of language in which the human mind has been so fertile in devising and borrowing abusive terms. In *The Female Eunuch,* Germaine Greer devotes four pages to anatomical terms and words for animals, vegetables, fruits, baked goods, implements, and receptacles, all of which are used to dehumanize the female person. Jean Faust, in an article aptly called "Words That Oppress," suggests that the effort to diminish women through language is rooted in a male fear of sexual inadequacy. "Woman is made to feel guilty for and akin to natural disasters," she writes; "hurricanes and typhoons are named after her. Any negative or threatening force is given a feminine name. If a man runs into bad luck climbing up the ladder of success (a male-invented game), he refers to the 'bitch goddess' success."

The sexual overtones in the ancient and no doubt honorable custom of calling ships "she" have become more explicit and less honorable in an age of air travel: "I'm Karen. Fly me." Attitudes of ridicule, contempt, and disgust toward female sexuality have spawned a rich glossary of insults and epithets not found in dictionaries. And the usage in which four-letter words meaning "copulate" are interchangeable with *cheat, attack,* and *destroy* can scarcely be unrelated to the savagery of rape.

In her updating of Ibsen's *A Doll's House,* Clare Booth Luce has Nora tell her husband she is pregnant—"In the way only men are supposed to get pregnant." "Men, pregnant?" he says, and she nods: "With ideas. Pregnancies there [*she taps his head*] are masculine. And a very superior form of labor. Pregnancies here [*taps her tummy*] are feminine—a very inferior form of labor."

Public outcry followed a revised translation of the New Testament describing Mary as "pregnant" instead of "great with child." The objections were made in part on aesthetic grounds: there is no attractive adjective in modern English for a woman who is about to give birth. A less obvious reason was that replacing the euphemism with a biological term undermined religious teaching. The initiative and generative power in the conception of Jesus are understood to be God's; Mary, the mother, was a vessel only.

Whether influenced by this teaching or not, the language of human reproduction lags several centuries behind scientific understanding. The male's contribution to procreation is still described as though it were the entire seed from which a new life grows: the initiative and generative power involved in the process are thought of as masculine, receptivity and nurturance as feminine. *Seminal* remains a synonym for "highly original," and there is no comparable word to describe the female's equivalent contribution.

An entire mythology has grown from this biological misunderstanding and its semantic legacy; its embodiment in laws that for centuries made women nonpersons was a key target of the nineteenth-century feminist movement. Today, more than fifty years after women finally won the basic democratic right to vote, the word *liberation* itself, when applied to women, means something less than when used of other groups of people. An advertisement for the NBC news department listed women's liberation along with crime in the streets and the Vietnam War as "bad news." Asked for his views on women's liberation, a highly placed politician was quoted as saying, "Let me make one thing perfectly clear. I wouldn't want to wake up next to a lady pipe-fitter."

One of the most surprising challenges to our male-dominated culture is coming from within organized religion, where the issues are being stated, in part, by confronting the implications of traditional language. What a growing number of theologians and scholars are saying is that the myths of the Judeo-Christian tradition, being the products of patriarchy, must be reexamined, and that the concept of an exclusively male ministry and the image of a male god have become idolatrous.

Women are naturally in the forefront of this movement, both in their efforts to gain ordination and full equality and through their contributions to theological reform, although both these efforts are often subtly diminished. When the Reverend Barbara Anderson was ordained by the American Lutheran Church, one newspaper printed her picture over a caption headed "Happy Girl." *Newsweek*'s report of a protest staged last December by women divinity students at Harvard was jocular ("another tilt at the windmill") and sarcastic: "Every time anyone in the room lapsed into what [the students] regarded as male chauvinism—such as using the word 'mankind' to describe the human race in general—the outraged women . . . drowned out the offender with earpiercing blasts from party-favor kazoos. . . . What annoyed the women most was the universal custom of referring to God as 'He.' "

The tone of the report was not merely unfunny; it missed the connection between increasingly outmoded theological language and the accelerating number of women (and men) who are dropping out of organized religion, both Jewish and Christian. For language, including pronouns, can be used to construct a reality that simply mirrors society's assumptions. To women who are committed to the reality of religious faith, the effect is doubly painful. Professor Harvey Cox, in whose classroom the protest took place, stated the issue directly: The women, he said, were raising the "basic theological question of whether God is more adequately thought of in personal or suprapersonal terms."

Toward the end of Don McLean's remarkable ballad "American Pie," a song filled with the imagery of abandonment and disillusion, there is a stanza that must strike many women to the quick. The church bells are broken, the music has died; then:

> And the three men I admire most,
> The Father, Son and the Holy Ghost,
> They caught the last train for the Coast—
> The day the music died.

Three men I admire most. There they go, briefcases in hand and topcoats buttoned left over right, walking down the long cold platform under the city, past the baggage wagons and the hissing steam onto the Pullman. Bye, bye, God—all three of you—made in the image of male supremacy. Maybe out there in L.A. where the weather is warmer, someone can believe in you again.

The Roman Catholic theologian Elizabeth Farians says "the bad theology of an overmasculinized church continues to be one of the root causes of women's oppression." The definition of oppression is "to crush or burden by abuse of power or authority; burden spiritually or mentally as if by pressure."

When language oppresses, it does so by any means that disparage and belittle. Until well into the twentieth century, one of the ways English was manipulated to disparage women was through the addition of feminine endings to nonsexual words. Thus a woman who aspired to be a poet was excluded from the company of real poets by the label *poetess,* and a woman who piloted an airplane was denied full status as an aviator by being called an *aviatrix.* At about the time *poetess, aviatrix,* and similar

Adam-ribbisms were dropping out of use, H. W. Fowler was urging that they be revived. "With the coming expansion of women's vocations," he wrote in the first edition (1926) of *Modern English Usage,* "feminines for vocation-words are a special need of the future." There can be no doubt he subconsciously recognized the relative status implied in the *-ess* designations. His criticism of a woman who wished to be known as an author rather than an authoress was that she had no need "to raise herself to the level of the male author by asserting her right to his name."

Who has the prior right to a name? The question has an interesting bearing on words that were once applied to men alone, or to both men and women, but now, having acquired abusive associations, are assigned to women exclusively. *Spinster* is a gentle case in point. *Prostitute* and many of its synonyms illustrate the phenomenon better. If Fowler had chosen to record the changing usage of *harlot* from "fellow" or "hired man" (in Chaucer's time) through "rascal" and "entertainer" to its present definition, would he have maintained that the female harlot is trying to raise herself to the level of the male harlot by asserting her right to his name? Or would he have plugged for *harlotress*?

The demise of most *-ess* endings came about before the start of the new feminist movement. In the second edition of *Modern English Usage,* published in 1965, Sir Ernest Gowers frankly admitted what his predecessors had been up to. "Feminine designations," he wrote, "seem now to be falling into disuse. Perhaps the explanation of this paradox is that it symbolizes the victory of women in their struggle for equal rights; it reflects the abandonment by men of those ideas about women in the professions that moved Dr. Johnson to his rude remark about women preachers."

If Sir Ernest's optimism can be justified, why is there a movement back to feminine endings in such words as *chairwoman, councilwoman,* and *congresswoman*? Betty Hudson, of Madison,

Connecticut, is campaigning for the adoption of *selectwoman* as the legal title for a female member of that town's executive body. To have to address a woman as "Selectman," she maintains, "is not only bad grammar and bad biology, but it implies that politics is still, or should be, a man's business." A valid argument, and one that was, predictably, countered by ridicule, the surefire weapon for undercutting achievement. When the head of the Federal Maritime Commission, Helen D. Bentley, was named "Man of the Year" by an association of shipping interests, she wisely refused to be drawn into light-hearted debate with interviewers who wanted to make the award's name a humorous issue. Some women, of course, have yet to learn they are invisible. An eight-year-old who visited the American Museum of Natural History with her Brownie scout troop went through the impressive exhibit on pollution and overpopulation called "Can Man Survive?" Asked afterward, "Well, can he?" she answered, "I don't know about him, but we're working on it in Brownies."

Nowhere are women rendered more invisible by language than in politics. The United States Constitution, in describing the qualifications for Representative, Senator, and President, refers to each as *he.* No wonder Shirley Chisholm, the first woman since 1888 to make a try for the Presidential nomination of a major party, found it difficult to be taken seriously.

The observation by Andrew Greeley already quoted—that "man" uses "his symbols" to reconstruct "his reality"—was not made in reference to the symbols of language but to the symbolic impact the "nomination of a black man for the Vice-Presidency" would have on race relations in the United States. Did the author assume the generic term *man* would of course be construed to include *woman*? Or did he deliberately use a semantic device to exclude Shirley Chisholm without having to be explicit?

Either way, his words construct a reality in which women are ignored. As much as any other factor in our language, the ambiguous meaning of *man* serves to deny women recognition as people. In a recent magazine article, we discussed the similar effect on women of the generic pronoun *he,* which we proposed to replace by a new common gender pronoun *tey.* We were immediately told, by a number of authorities, that we were dabbling in the serious business of linguistics, and the message that reached us from these scholars was loud and clear: It-is-absolutely-impossible- for- anyone- to- introduce- a- new- word- into- the-language-just-because-there-is-a-need-for-it, so-stop-wasting-your-time.

When words are suggested like "sportsoneship" (for *sportsmanship*) and "mistresspiece" (for the work of a Virginia Woolf) one suspects a not-too-subtle attempt to make the whole language problem look silly. But unless Alexander Pope, when he wrote, "The proper study of mankind is man," meant that women should be relegated to the footnotes (or, as George Orwell might have put it, "All men are equal, but men are more equal than women"), viable new words will surely someday supersede the old.

Without apologies to Freud, the great majority of women do not wish in their hearts that they were men. If having grown up with a language that tells them they are at the same time men and not men raises psychic doubts for women, the doubts are not of their sexual identity but of their human identity. Perhaps the present unrest surfacing in the women's movement is part of an evolutionary change in our particular form of life—the one form of all in the animal and plant kingdoms that orders and interprets its reality by symbols. The achievements of the species called man have brought us to the brink of self-destruction. If the species survives into the next century with the expectation of going on, it may only be because we have become part of what Harlow Shapley calls the psychozoic kingdom, where brain overshadows brawn and rationality has replaced superstition.

Searching the roots of Western civilization for a word to call this new species of man and woman, someone might come up with *gen,* as in *genesis* and *generic.* With such a word, *man* could be used exclusively for males as *woman* is used for females, for *gen* would include both sexes. Like the words *deer* and *bison, gen* would be both plural and singular. Like *progenitor, progeny,* and *generation,* it would convey continuity. *Gen* would express the warmth and generalized sexuality of *generous, gentle,* and *genuine;* the specific sexuality of *genital* and *genetic.* In the new family of gen, girls and boys would grow to genhood, and to speak of genkind would be to include all the people of the earth.

NOTES

PREFACE TO THE ORIGINAL EDITION

1. Lynn White, Jr., "The Changing Canons of Our Culture," in *Frontiers of Knowledge in the Study of Man,* Lynn White, Jr., ed., New York, Harper & Bros., 1956, p. 308.

CHAPTER 1 BEGINNING WITH NAMES

1. The recruitment ad appeared in the September 30, 1974, issue of *Time* magazine, pp. 84–85. By the following year, similar ads were posed in such a way that the name of each recruit was visible.

2. Helen Keller, *The Story of My Life,* Garden City, N.Y., Doubleday & Company, 1955, p. 36. (First published in 1902.)

3. Eric H. Lenneberg, "On Explaining Language," *Science,* May 9, 1969, pp. 635–43.

4. Ethel Strainchamps, "Our Sexist Language," in Vivian Gornick and Barbara K. Moran, eds., *Woman in Sexist Society,* New York, Basic Books, 1971, p. 247.

5. The study by James Bruning and William Albott, reported in the March 1974 issue of *Human Behavior,* was described by Melvin Maddocks, the Christian Science Monitor News Service, and reprinted in the *Middletown* (Conn.) *Press,* June 26, 1974.

6. Linwood Sleigh and Charles Johnson, *Apollo Book of Girls' Names,* New York, Thomas Y. Crowell Company, 1962, p. 194.

7. Alice H. Bonnell, "Women at Columbia: The Long March to Equal Opportunities," *Columbia Reports,* May 1972.

8. University of North Carolina News Bureau press release reprinted in the university's *Alumni Review,* November 1971.

9. Based on figures reported in *The World Almanac & Book of Facts 1990,* New York, Newspaper Enterprise Association, 1989.

10. "Booklet for Women Who Wish to Determine Their Own Names After Marriage," Barrington, Ill., Center for a Woman's Own Name, 1974, p. 7.

11. Quoted by Carmen Rubio in "Staying Single—In Name Only," *Sunday, The Hartford Courant Magazine,* February 2, 1975.

12. Stephen Birmingham, *The Right People: A Portrait of the American Social Establishment,* Boston, Little, Brown and Company, 1968, p. 9.

13. "Newsline," *Psychology Today,* August 1974, p. 29.

14. Robert T. Means, Jr., Letter to the Editor, *Psychology Today,* November 1974, p. 14.

15. Elizabeth Janeway, *Man's World, Woman's Place: A Study in Social Mythology,* New York, A Delta Book, Dell Publishing Company, 1971, p. 37.

16. Mike McGrady, "Family Banking," *New York* magazine, June 12, 1972, p. 42.

17. Otto Weininger, *Sex and Character,* New York, G. P. Putnam's Sons, 1906, p. 206. This is the "authorized translation from the sixth German edition"; also published in London by William Heinemann.

18. Ibid., p. 286.

19. Quoted by Lucy Komisar, *The New Feminism,* New York, Warner Paperback Library, 1971, p. 81. Blackstone's *Commentaries* was first published in 1765–69.

20. Arline Brecher, "Male Lib: The Men Who Want Human Liberation: An Interview with Psychologist Jack Sawyer," *New Woman,* February 1972, p. 75.

21. Jean Stafford, "Don't Use Ms. with Miss Stafford, Unless You Mean ms.," *New York Times,* September 21, 1973, p. 36.

22. Ellen Cohn, "The Liberated Woman," *New York Sunday News* magazine, June 17, 1973, p. 4.

23. Pauli Murray, testimony before Rep. Edith Green's Special Subcommittee on Education in Support of Section 805 of H.R. 16098, June 19, 1970, U.S. Government Printing Office, 1970.

24. Except for the final paragraph, the arguments in this section are drawn from Phyllis Trible, "Depatriarchalizing in Biblical Interpretation," *Journal of the American Academy of Religion,* March 1973, Vol. 41, No. 1, pp. 35–42. We are indebted to Rabbi A. James Rudin of the American Jewish Committee for the following additional comment: "The root Hebrew word for 'ADAM' is 'ADAMAH' (soil or earth). 'ADAMAH' is a feminine noun, and it could be argued that 'ADAM' is a derivation both linguistically and symbolically from an archtype 'Mother Earth' Hebrew concept."

CHAPTER 2 WHO IS MAN?

1. J. Bronowski, *The Ascent of Man,* Boston, Little, Brown and Company, 1973, p. 24.

2. The *Middletown* (Conn.) *Press,* November 27, 1972.

3. Joseph W. Schneider and Sally L. Hacker, "Sex Role Imagery and the Use of the Generic 'Man' in Introductory Texts: A Case in the Sociology of Sociology," paper presented at the section on Sociology of Sex Roles, American Sociological Association Annual Meetings, August 1972, New Orleans. The paper was published in *American Sociologist,* February 1973, pp. 12–18.

4. Letter from Schneider and Hacker, summarizing the results of their study, sent to over one hundred publishers of sociology titles, April 19, 1972.

5. Sally L. Hacker, Phyllis Blood, and Joseph Schneider, "Further Notes on Cultural and Structural Oppression of Women: Man's Language and His Publishing Houses." Photocopy, no date.

6. Of eight dictionaries for young people consulted, only one, The Weekly Reader Beginning Dictionary, Grades 2 and 3 (William Morris, ed., New York, Grosset & Dunlap, 1974) defines *man* as "people in general" in addition to man as an adult male. The example provided was, "Man has invented many things to make life easy."

7. The Golden Picture Dictionary for Beginning Readers, New York, Golden Press, 1972 edition, Western Publishing Company, Racine, Wis.

8. Alleen Pace Nilsen, "Grammatical Gender and Its Relationship to the Equal Treatment of Males and Females in Children's Books," Ph.D. diss., University of Iowa, 1973, pp. 106–7, 121–32.

9. Ibid., p. 96.

10. Linda Harrison, "Cro-Magnon Woman—In Eclipse," *The Science Teacher,* April 1975, pp. 8–11.

11. Ibid., p. 11.

12. Erich Fromm, "The Erich Fromm Theory of Aggression," *New York Times Magazine,* February 27, 1972.

13. The ad appeared in *Time* magazine, October 4, 1971.

14. Quoted by Marjorie Anderson and Blanche Williams, *Old English Handbook,* Boston, Houghton Mifflin Company, 1935, p. 207.

15. Both examples are given under the entry *man* in the Oxford English Dictionary. For convenience we have modernized the spelling.

16. Alma Graham, "How to Make Trouble: The Making of a Nonsexist Dictionary," *Ms.,* December 1973, p. 16.

17. Nilsen, op. cit., pp. 86–87.

18. Patricia C. Nichols, "The Uses of Gender in English," revision of a paper read before the Women's Forum of the Modern Language Association in December 1971 under the title "Gender in English: Syntactic and Semantic Functions"; photocopy, p. 11.

19. Nilsen, op. cit., pp. 16, 17.

20. Ibid., p. 18.

21. Gene Shalit, on the "Today Show," NBC Television, October 23, 1974.

22. The Quaker Oats Company, Chicago, Ill., on packets containing maple and brown sugar oatmeal.

23. "Plastic Monster Being Readied to Lure Nessie," *Manchester Guardian* news item reprinted in the *Middletown* (Conn.) *Press,* June 7, 1975.

24. Benjamin Spock, M.D., *Redbook,* November 1973, as quoted in *Today's Education,* September–October 1974, p. 110.

25. Lee Salk, *Preparing for Parenthood,* New York, David McKay Company, 1974.

26. James D. McCawley, Letter to the Editor, *New York Times Magazine,* November 10, 1974.

27. Ibid.

28. Alma Graham, Letter to the Editor, *The Columbia Forum,* Fall 1974.

29. Gena Corea, "Frankly Feminist," syndicated column dated June 28, 1974, reprinted in *Media Report to Women,* Vol. 3, No. 1, January 1, 1975.

30. *Today's Education,* September–October 1974, p. 110.

31. Theodore M. Bernstein, *The Careful Writer: A Modern Guide to English Usage,* New York, Atheneum, 1965, and *Watch Your Language,* Great Neck, N.Y., Channel Press, 1958; Peter Farb, *Word Play: What Happens When People Talk,* New York, Alfred A. Knopf, 1974.

32. Ethel Strainchamps, review of Peter Farb, *Word Play,* in *The Village Voice, Voice Literary Supplement,* March 21, 1974. Examples are cited by the Oxford English Dictionary under entries for *they, their, them,* and *themselves.*

33. The Abigail Adams letter of 31 March 1776, and John Adams's reply of 14 April 1776, are quoted from Miriam Schneir, ed., *Feminism: The Essential Historical Writings,* New York, Vintage Books, 1972, pp. 3–4.

34. Volume 10, p. 48B, 1971 edition. The Britannica Junior Encyclopædia for Boys and Girls is compiled with the editorial advice of the Faculties of the University of Chicago and the University Laboratory Schools and published by Encyclopædia Britannica, Inc.

35. Jacques Barzun, "A Few Words on a Few Words," *The Columbia Forum,* Summer 1974, p. 19.

36. Frank McGee, on the "Today Show," NBC Television, June 16, 1972.

37. Theodore Caplow, *Elementary Sociology,* Englewood Cliffs, N.J., Prentice-Hall, 1971, p. 310, quoted by Schneider and Hacker, "Sex Role Imagery," fn. 9.

38. Justine DeLacy, "How French Women Got That Way—And How to Handle Them," *New York Times,* January 13, 1974, "Travel and Resorts" section.

39. Robert H. Bork, "We Suddenly Feel That Law Is Vulnerable," *Fortune* magazine, December 1971.

40. Richard P. Goldwater, M.D., Letter to the Editor, *The Columbia Forum,* Fall 1974, p. 46.

CHAPTER 3 SEX AND GENDER

1. Quoted without source by Theodore Lidz in *The Person: His Development throughout the Life Cycle,* New York, Basic Books, 1968, pp. 61–62 fn., as "an example, more amusing than malignant, of the handicaps imposed upon a child by cultural deprivation."

2. Nilsen, "Grammatical Gender and Its Relationship to the Equal Treatment of Males and Females in Children's Books," p. 77.

3. Mark Twain, "The Awful German Language," from *A Tramp Abroad,* reprinted in *The Family Mark Twain,* New York, Harper & Brothers, 1935, pp. 1147–48.

4. Ibid., pp. 1148, 1149.

5. George Lyman Kittredge and Frank Edgar Farley, *A Concise English Grammar,* Boston, Ginn and Company, 1918, p. 22.

6. Lynn White, Jr., *Frontiers of Knowledge,* p. 307.

7. H. W. Fowler, *A Dictionary of Modern English Usage,* New York, Oxford University Press, 1950, under the entry "Feminine Designations," p. 176.

8. Ibid.

9. Oxford English Dictionary, under the entry *-er.* For convenience, we have spelled out abbreviations occurring in the OED in all quotations from it that follow.

10. Ibid., under the entry *-ster.*

11. Ibid., under the entry *-ess.*

12. Ibid., under the entry *-ster.*

13. Barbara Ehrenreich and Deirdre English, "Witches, Midwives, and Nurses: A History of Women Healers," Oyster Bay, N.Y., Glass Mountain Pamphlets, n.d., p. 18.

14. Oxford English Dictionary, under the entry *-ess.*

15. Fowler, loc. cit.

16. The earliest reference to *actress* in the OED is dated 1700. According to the Columbia Encyclopedia, women began acting on the English stage in 1656. In 1666 Samuel Pepys wrote of a woman that she "will be an excellent actor, I think."

17. Personal correspondence with Rhoda B. Jenkins.

18. Mary Douglas, ed., *Rules and Meanings: The Anthropology of Everyday Knowledge,* Baltimore, Penguin Education, 1973, p. 117.

19. Jan Morris, *Conundrum,* New York, Harcourt Brace Jovanovich, 1974, as excerpted in *Ms.,* July 1974, pp. 57, 60.

CHAPTER 4 SEMANTIC POLARIZATION

1. Calvert Watkins, "Indo-European and the Indo-Europeans," in the American Heritage Dictionary of the English Language, New York, American Heritage Publishing Company, 1969, p. 1498.

2. Theodore Lidz, *The Person: His Development throughout the Life Cycle,* New York, Basic Books, 1968, pp. 60, 62.

3. Theodore Lidz, *The Person: His and Her Development throughout the Life Cycle,* rev. ed., New York, Basic Books, 1983, p. 62. The use of gender-inclusive language in this passage contrasts significantly with the wording used in the 1968 edition of *The Person.* In the first edition, quoted in earlier printings of *Words and Women,* the passage read as follows:

> Language is the means by which man internalizes his experience, thinks about it, tries out alternatives, conceptualizes a future and strives toward future goals. . . . Indeed, the capacity to direct the self into the future, which we shall term "ego functioning," depends upon a person having verbal symbols with which he constructs an internalized symbolic version of the world which he can manipulate in imaginative trial and error before committing himself to irrevocable actions *etc*. . . .

In a 1989 article published in *The Journal of the American Medical Women's Association,* two psychiatrists discuss the implications of false generics in scientific and medical writing. They quote statements from Dr. Lidz's chapter "The Oedipal Period" as it read in the original edition of *The Person,* and they comment: "Here the author's use of 'he' to refer to a child of either sex sets the stage for a discussion of the oedipal rivalry from a boy's point of view only, and readers must extrapolate on their own to understand such rivalry from a girl's perspective." Referring to the revised edition, they note, "Here the explanation of similar material gains richness and accuracy with nonsexist phrasing and without false generics." Susan Schneider, M.D., and Ana Maria Soto, M.D., "Sexist Language: Should We Be Concerned?" JAMWA, Vol. 44, No. 3, May/June 1989.

4. Watkins, loc. cit.

5. Quoted by Enid Nemy, "Violent Crime by Young People: No Easy Answer," *New York Times,* March 17, 1975.

6. William Safire, "A Cap Over the Wall," *New York Times,* July 5, 1973. He refers to a poem by Kipling, better forgotten.

7. The study was reported in Ruth E. Hartley, "Sex-Role Pressures and the Socialization of the Male Child," *Psychological Reports,* Vol. 5, 1959, pp. 457–68, and the quotations and conclusions are all drawn from that article.

8. Quoted by Betty Friedan, *The Feminine Mystique,* New York, Dell Publishing Company, 1970, p. 75. (First published in 1963.)

9. Oxford English Dictionary, under the entry *shrew.*

10. Alleen and Don Nilsen, "Ms. and Mr. Nilsen Debate Sexism in English," transcript of a presentation made at a National Council of Teachers of English meeting, November 23, 1973.

11. Oxford English Dictionary, under the entry *tomboy.*

12. The incidents described occurred on a state college campus in Connecticut in December 1973 and January 1974.

13. Juli Loesch, "Testeria and Penisolence—A Scourge to Humankind," *Aphra: The Feminist Literary Magazine,* Vol. 4, No. 1, Winter 1972–73, pp. 43–45.

14. Margaret Mead, *Sex and Temperament in Three Primitive Societies,* New York, Dell Publishing Company, Laurel Edition, 1968, p. 281. (First published in 1935.) Susan Brownmiller, in her landmark study of rape, *Against Our Will: Men, Women and Rape,* New York, Simon & Schuster, 1975, explores the effects of socially assigned aggressor and victim sex roles. In discussing Alan J. Davis's study of sexual assault among males in prison, Brownmiller says: "Davis found that prison rape was a product of the violent subculture's *definition of masculinity through physical triumph,* and those who emerged as 'women' were those who were subjugated by real or threatened force" (p. 267, emphasis added).

15. Mead, *Sex and Temperament,* p. 286. For a helpful analysis of what the word *normal* has come to mean with reference to human females and males, see Ruth Herschberger, *Adam's Rib,* note 1 to Chapter 1 (pp. 203–12 in the paperback edition published by Harper & Row).

16. The incident described took place on October 18, 1973, on a field trip for New York City school children at the Croton River conducted by the Wave Hill Center for Environmental Studies.

17. Friedan, op. cit., p. 145.

18. Mead, op. cit., p. 278.

CHAPTER 5 THE LANGUAGE OF RELIGION

1. Quoted by Robert H. Thouless, *Authority and Freedom: Some Psychological Problems of Religious Belief,* London, Hodder and Stoughton, 1954, p. 78.

2. This and the following quotations and information on the Aztec language are from Mary Ritchie Key, *Male/Female Language,* Metuchen, N.J., Scarecrow Press, 1974, pp. 20–21.

3. Phyllis Trible, "Depatriarchalizing in Biblical Interpretation," pp. 35–36.

4. Ibid. See also Russell C. Prohl, *Concerning the Ordination of Women,* Geneva, World Council of Churches, 1964, p. 30, quoted in Emily C. Hewitt and Suzanne R. Hiatt, *Women Priests: Yes or No?* New York, The Seabury Press, 1973, p. 52.

5. We are indebted for this analysis to Phyllis Trible, who discusses the female imagery of Deuteronomy 32:18 in her article "God, Nature of in the

Old Testament" in *The Interpreter's Dictionary of the Bible: Supplementary Volume,* Nashville, Abingdon Press, 1976. This article and Dr. Trible's paper "Depatriarchalizing in Biblical Interpretation," cited in Chapter 1, note 24, provide numerous other instances of female imagery for God in the Bible.

6. See footnote *j,* p. 125 of the 1946 edition of the Revised Standard Version of the New Testament, New York, Thomas Nelson & Sons.

7. Ruth Hoppin, "Games Bible Translators Play," six-page photocopy © 1972 by Ruth Hoppin, p. 1.

8. Krister Stendahl, "Enrichment or Threat? When the Eves Come Marching In," in *Sexist Religion and Women in the Church: No More Silence!* Alice L. Hageman, ed., in collaboration with the Women's Caucus of Harvard Divinity School, New York, Association Press, 1974, pp. 120–21. Dean Stendahl's address was delivered as part of a 1972–73 lecture series on women and religion.

9. E. J. Dionne, "Two Women Liberate Church Course," *The Harvard Crimson,* November 11, 1971.

10. "Pronoun Envy," *Newsweek,* December 6, 1971, p. 58.

11. Ibid.

12. *The Harvard Crimson,* November 16, 1971, p. 17.

13. James Armagost, Letter to the Editor, *Newsweek,* December 27, 1971.

14. Randall Blake Michael, ibid.

15. C. Kilmer Myers, "Should Women Be Ordained?" *The Episcopalian,* February 1972, p. 8.

16. *Children's Letters to God,* compiled by Eric Marshall and Stuart Hample, New York, Pocket Books, 1966, unpaged.

17. Thouless, op. cit., pp. 71–72.

18. The remark was made at the Conference of Women Theologians sponsored by the Research Center on Women, Alverno College, Milwaukee, Wis., June 7–18, 1971, and reported in "Transcription of the Opening Session," photocopy, p. 15.

19. Earle Fox, *The Bell Ringer,* St. Stephen's Episcopal Church, East Haddam, Conn., February 27, 1972.

20. Mary Ellmann, *Thinking About Women,* New York, Harcourt Brace Jovanovich, 1968, pp. 5–6. At the time Ellmann wrote, all U.S. astronauts were male.

21. Oxford English Dictionary, under the entry *mortmain.*

22. "Notes," Conference of Women Theologians, June 1971, Research Center on Women, Alverno College, photocopy, p. 2.

23. Ibid., pp. 11, 12.

24. Mary Daly, *Beyond God the Father: Toward a Philosophy of Women's Liberation,* Boston, Beacon Press, 1973, p. 47.

25. Ibid., pp. 8, 37.

26. Mary Daly, "The End of God the Father," *The Unitarian Universalist*

Christian, Fall/Winter 1972, as reprinted and excerpted in *Intellectual Digest,* May 1973.

27. Daly, *Beyond God the Father,* p. 189.

CHAPTER 6 THE GREAT MALE PLOT

1. Stefan Kanfer, "Sispeak: A Msguided Attempt to Change Herstory," *Time* magazine, October 23, 1972, p. 79.
2. Diane B. Schulder, "Does the Law Oppress Women?" in Robin Morgan, ed., *Sisterhood Is Powerful,* New York, Vintage Books, 1970, p. 148.
3. "Guidelines for Improving the Image of Women in Textbooks," Glenview, Ill., Scott, Foresman and Company, 1972, p. 5.
4. William F. Buckley, Jr., "On the Right: Who's Beautiful?" *Middletown* (Conn.) *Press,* November 30, 1972.
5. Ibid.
6. George F. Will, "Sexist Guidelines and Reality," *Washington Post,* September 20, 1974.
7. Ibid.
8. Kanfer, loc. cit.
9. Russell Baker, "Observer: Nopersonclature," *New York Times,* March 4, 1973.
10. Personal correspondence with Alma Graham.
11. Roger W. Westcott, "Women, Wife-Men, and Sexist Bias," *Verbatim: The Language Quarterly,* September 1974, p. 1.
12. Otto Jespersen, *Language: Its Nature Development and Origin,* New York, Henry Holt and Company, 1922, p. 249.
13. William W. Hallo and J. J. A. van Dijk, *The Exaltation of Inanna,* New Haven, Conn., Yale University Press, 1968, p. 1. The authors identify Enheduanna, who lived in Sumeria c. 2300 B.C., as the first authenticated poet in history. Her cycle of hymns to Inanna resulted in the latter's cultic primacy in Ur and Uruk.
14. Lincoln Barnett, *The Treasure of Our Tongue,* New York, Alfred A. Knopf, 1964, p. 97.
15. Mary R. Beard, *Woman as Force in History: A Study in Traditions and Realities,* New York, The Macmillan Company, 1946, pp. 183, 192, and *passim.*
16. Quoted by George H. McKnight, *The Evolution of the English Language from Chaucer to the Twentieth Century,* New York, Dover Publications, 1968, pp. 100–2. (First published in 1928.)
17. Margaret Lawrence, *The School of Femininity,* New York, Frederick A. Stokes Company, 1936, pp. 3–4.
18. Virginia Woolf, *A Room of One's Own,* New York, Harcourt, Brace and Company, 1929, pp. 80–84.

19. Edward B. Jenkinson, *What Is Language?* Bloomington, Ind., Indiana University Press, 1967, p. 176.

20. Ernest Weekley, "On Dictionaries," *The Atlantic Monthly,* June 1924, pp. 782–91, as reprinted in James Sledd and Wilma R. Ebbitt, *Dictionaries and* That *Dictionary,* Chicago, Scott, Foresman and Company, 1962, p. 13.

21. Thomas Pyles, *The Origins and Development of the English Language,* New York, Harcourt, Brace & World, 1964, p. 213.

22. Quoted by Barnett, op. cit., p. 183.

23. Barnett, op. cit., p. 218.

24. Quoted by Sir Ernest Gowers in his introduction to H. W. Fowler, *A Dictionary of Modern English Usage,* 2nd ed., revised by Sir Ernest Gowers, London, Clarendon Press, 1965, p. iii.

25. Fowler, *A Dictionary of Modern English Usage,* New York, Oxford University Press, 1950, p. 392.

26. The quotations are from Gowers's introduction to Fowler, 2nd ed., p. viii.

27. *Life* magazine, October 27, 1961, p. 4, as reprinted in Sledd and Ebbitt, op. cit., p. 85.

28. Garry Wills, *The National Review,* February 13, 1962, pp. 98–99, as reprinted in Sledd and Ebbitt, op. cit., p. 131.

29. Millicent Taylor, *Christian Science Monitor,* November 29, 1961, and Ethel Strainchamps, *Saint Louis Post-Dispatch,* October 29, 1961, and December 17, 1961.

30. Robert Gordon Latham, *A Dictionary of the English Language,* London, Longmans, Green and Company, 1876. This is a revision of the Rev. H. J. Todd's 1818 edition of Samuel Johnson's dictionary.

31. Quoted by Fern Marja Eckman, "Check One," *New York Post Magazine,* January 19, 1974, p. 5.

32. George Gilder, *Sexual Suicide,* New York, Quadrangle/The New York Times Book Company, 1973, p. 21 and *passim.*

33. Reported by Jennifer Chatfield who attended the 1975 hearings in Albany.

34. *Brunswick* (Me.) *Times-Record,* May 16, 1974.

35. As reported in *Media Report to Women,* January 1, 1974, p. 11. The *Times* had announced its change in policy with respect to *Mr.* on November 22, 1973. In June 1986, the *Times* announced that it would henceforth permit the use of *Ms.* as a courtesy title, commenting editorially, "The Times now believes that 'Ms.' has become part of the language."

36. *New York Times,* May 16, 1974.

37. Ellen Cohn, speaking May 12, 1974, at the [*MORE*] Convention in New York, as reported in *Media Report to Women,* June 1, 1974. The *Times* story Cohn cited was dated January 16, 1974.

38. Cohn, loc. cit.

39. Robert J. Leeney, "Editor's Note: Women and the News," *New Haven Register,* April 13, 1974, p. 14.

40. "Bernstein on Words," *Philadelphia Bulletin,* as reported by S. P. Norse in a Letter to the Editor, *New York Times,* March 21, 1974.

41. Russell Baker, "Observer: Murm and Smur," *Middletown* (Conn.) *Press,* November 3, 1971.

42. Pauli Murray, testimony before Rep. Edith Green's Special Subcommittee on Education in Support of Section 805 of H.R. 16098, June 19, 1970, U.S. Government Printing Office, 1970, p. 330; Cohn, loc. cit.; Stephanie Harrington, "Women Get the Short End of the Shtick," *New York Times,* November 18, 1973, "Arts and Leisure" section, p. 21.

CHAPTER 7 WHAT IS WOMAN?

1. Weininger, *Sex and Character,* p. 92.

2. Alfred Adler, *Understanding Human Nature,* New York, Greenberg Publisher, 1946, pp. 123, 257. (First published in 1927.) We are indebted to Jo-Ann Evans Gardner for bringing these quotations to our attention.

3. *The Virginia Gazette,* October 22, 1736, as quoted by Edmund S. Morgan, *Virginians at Home: Family Life in the Eighteenth Century,* Williamsburg, Va., Colonial Williamsburg, 1952, p. 38.

4. *New York Times,* April 24, 1974.

5. Personal communication with Kathleen Pietrunti.

6. Frank Williams cartoon, *Detroit Free Press,* reprinted in *Time* magazine, May 20, 1974.

7. Louise Sweeney, "Pretty Lawyer Sharp as a Tack," *Middletown* (Conn.) *Press,* April 3, 1975, p. 11.

8. Transcript of "Firing Line" originally broadcast on PBS, April 6, 1975.

9. Robin Lakoff, "Language and Woman's Place," photocopy sent by the author to Miller and Swift, January 1973. The article was later published in *Language in Society,* Vol. 2, April 1973, and appeared in the author's *Language and Woman's Place,* New York, Harper & Row, 1975.

10. Lakoff, photocopy, p. 3.

11. Ibid., p. 4.

12. Gunnar Myrdal, *An American Dilemma,* New York, Harper & Brothers, 1944, Appendix 5.

13. Key, *Male/Female Language,* pp. 104, 105.

14. Otto Jespersen, *Language: Its Nature Development and Origin,* pp. 246–47.

15. Morris L. Ernst, Foreword to James Joyce, *Ulysses,* New York, The Modern Library, 1940, p. vii.

16. Strainchamps, "Our Sexist Language," pp. 248–49.

17. Ibid., p. 249.

18. Lawrence Stessin, "Women Are Breaking the Blue-Collar Barrier," *New York Times,* August 26, 1973, "Business and Finance" section, p. 3.

19. Contemporary lexicographic treatment of formerly forbidden sex words is humorously described by Sidney I. Landau in "*sexual intercourse* in American College Dictionaries," *Verbatim,* Vol. 1, No. 1, 1974.

20. *An Intelligent Woman's Guide to Dirty Words,* Volume 1 of the Feminist English Dictionary, Chicago, Loop Center YWCA, 1973, p. ii.

21. Ibid., pp. iv–v.

22. "CBS Morning News," August 18, 1973, Hughes Rudd speaking to Sally Quinn.

23. Barbara Lawrence, "Dirty Words *Can* Harm You," *Redbook,* May 1974, p. 33.

24. Ibid.

25. Strainchamps, "Our Sexist Language," p. 244.

26. Reported by Ethel Strainchamps, "Ethel Strainchamps Wrote This," *New York Times,* October 4, 1971, p. 39.

27. Clayton Riley, "Did O. J. Dance?" *Ms.,* March 1974, p. 98.

28. Hartley, "Sex-Role Pressures," p. 462.

29. Elinor P. O'Connor, Complainant vs. Lum, Biunno and Tompkins, Respondent, State of New Jersey, Department of Law and Safety, Division on Civil Rights, Docket No. AG145B033, "Memorandum on Use of the Word 'Bitch,' " [1972].

30. Ibid., p. 4.

31. Joreen, "The Bitch Manifesto," Pittsburgh, KNOW, Inc., n.d., p. 3.

32. Strainchamps, "The Origins of Obscenity," [*MORE*] *A Journalism Review,* July 1972, p. 10.

33. "As the inflectional endings of Old English words were sloughed off, the word roots began to bear more semantic weight. As a result, there was a surge of alterations in the pronunciations and the meanings of words in the existing lexicon, born of an impulse to make the words fit the growing consensus on phonetic semantics. The most thoroughly documented of these changes have been those involving the vowels pronounced with a rounded mouth. In nouns, the oral aperture used in pronouncing these vowels was obviously felt to be gestural; it implied that the thing referred to was round or surrounding, the round things including orifices and living things. In inanimate nouns, the size of the aperture corresponded to the relative size of the referent. Thus we have *crock, bowl, spoon, cup, hook.* In animate nouns, the size of the vowel corresponded to the status of the referent (*God, father, cock; pope, soldier, scrotum; beauty, fool, womb; mother, dunce, cunt; woman, crook, foot*).

"Besides the vowels in the preceding sequence, in which size/status and vowel size were equated, four other vocalic phonemes acquired a gender sense: long *i* (masculine/high-status); and *ow, aw,* and radical *er* (feminine/low-status). Before the shift began, *mother, daughter,* and *nurse* had long *o*'s; *girl* was sexually inclusive; *child* was feminine; *shrew* and *bawd* were masculine. Gender exceptions fall into classes: e.g., *wife, bride, concubine, dyke; whore, widow, bimbo, crone, coed; suitor, groom, eunuch, fruit; husband, lover, cuckold*—all are other-sex-defined; the masculine consonants of *brother, bull,* etc. (*b* plus *r* or *l*) counteract their feminine vowels." Condensed by Ethel Strainchamps from her unpublished article "The Story of O and OO: Hidden Gender in English," 1976.

34. Strainchamps, "The Origins of Obscenity," p. 10.

35. The incident was reported to the authors by John Taylor, a field representative of the American Red Cross during the Second World War.

36. Nan Blitman and Robin Green, "Inez Garcia on Trial," *Ms.,* May 1975, p. 85; Lacey Fosburgh, "Trial Raises Questions on Rape Victims' Rights," *New York Times,* October 3, 1974.

37. James Reston, Jr., "The Joan Little Case," *New York Times Magazine,* April 6, 1975, p. 45.

38. Dr. Vladimir Piskacek, a psychiatrist, was quoted to this effect in "X-Rated Expletives," *Time* magazine, May 20, 1974. The function of taboo words for sexual intercourse was also discussed by Allen Walker Read in "An Obscenity Symbol," *American Speech,* December 1934, Vol. 9, No. 4. Professor Read recorded the history of "the most disreputable of all English words" (presumably the publication would have been banned from the mails had he spelled it out) and commented that such words serve "as scapegoats, ministering to the deep-rooted need for symbols of the forbidden." He suggested that those who wish to "take up the cudgels for the improvement of humanity" should go about it "not by suppressing these four-letter words, but by cleansing them through use in a nonpornographic manner." He did not, however, comment on the use of the same four-letter words to express contempt and hostility.

39. Gilder, *Sexual Suicide,* p. 259.

40. Nancy Chodorow, "Being and Doing," in *Women in Sexist Society,* p. 193.

41. Friedan, *The Feminine Mystique,* pp. 255, 351.

CHAPTER 8 THE SPECTER OF UNISEX

1. Blake Green, "A New English: Unbiased or Unsexed?" *San Francisco Chronicle,* October 11, 1974, p. 23.

2. William Strunk, Jr., *The Elements of Style,* rev. and with an introduction by E. B. White, New York, The Macmillan Company, Macmillan Paperbacks, 1959, p. 70.

3. David B. Wilson, "His/hers," *Boston Globe,* May 24, 1975, p. 7.

4. Jacques Barzun, "A Few Words on a Few Words," p. 17.

5. Ruth Schwartz Cowan, Letter to the Editor, *The Columbia Forum,* Fall 1974, inside front cover.

6. Common Cause, "Report from Washington," February 1975, p. 3.

7. American Association for the Advancement of Science, "Bulletin," June 1974, pp. 3, 5–12.

8. Personal correspondence with Connecticut State Senator Betty Hudson.

9. Michael Regan, "Woman Senator Waging Fight on Stereotyping," *Hartford Courant,* April 21, 1975, p. 2.

10. "California Voters Pamphlet, General Election, November 5, 1974," Proposition 11, pp. 40–43; *Hartford Courant,* November 7, 1974, p. 4.

11. American Anthropological Association, "Newsletter," January 1974, p. 12.

12. Frederick Cusick, "Law Students Win Their Case—Against a Will," *Daily Hampshire Gazette* (Northampton, Mass.), March 1, 1975, and personal correspondence.

13. Bradford W. O'Hearn, "N.Y. Kiwanis Club Admits First Woman," *Middletown* (Conn.) *Press,* January 23, 1974; "Kiwanis Trustees Tell Club to Drop Women Members," ibid., February 8, 1974; personal communication with Florence Bromley, Great Neck Kiwanis Club member, February 6, 1975.

14. Mary Orovan, "Humanizing English," 3rd ed., Hackensack, N.J., Art and Copy, 1972 (first published in 1970); personal correspondence with Orovan and with a member of the Twin Oaks Community.

15. We are indebted to Caldwell Titcomb of Brandeis University for bringing the existence of *thon* to our attention. For some years Professor Titcomb conducted a letter-writing campaign on behalf of Converse's proposal.

16. Carol L. O'Neill and Avima Ruder, *The Complete Guide to Editorial Freelancing,* New York, Dodd, Mead & Company, 1974, p. 1 n.

17. "Experts Tell Sirica That the Gap in Tape Was Due to Erasures," *New York Times,* January 16, 1974, p. 16.

18. WTIC-TV evening news, Channel 3, Hartford, Conn., May 25, 1971.

19. State of Connecticut, "An Act Requiring Counseling Prior to Abortion," Proposed Bill No. 263, General Assembly, January Session, 1975.

20. *Knoxville* (Tenn.) *Daily Beacon,* May 29, 1973, pp. 1, 4.

21. "Student Newspaper Is Abolishing Sex," Reuters dispatch in *Kitchener-Waterloo* (Ont.) *Record,* May 30, 1973; also carried by the *Los Angeles Times, New York Times,* and other newspapers.

22. Personal correspondence with Gary Moore, Publications Board, University of Tennessee.

23. George Orwell, "Politics and the English Language," from *Shoot-*

ing an Elephant and Other Essays, New York, Harcourt, Brace & World, 1950, as reprinted in James F. Hoy and John Somer, eds., *The Language Experience,* New York, Dell Publishing Company, A Delta Original, 1974, p. 115.

24. George Orwell, *Nineteen Eighty-Four,* New York, Harcourt, Brace and Company, 1949, p. 53.

25. Ibid., Appendix, "The Principles of Newspeak," p. 304.

26. Kanfer, "Sispeak."

27. Orwell, "The Principles of Newspeak," p. 310.

28. Ibid., p. 311.

29. Ann Sheldon, Letter to the Editor, *Yale Alumni Magazine,* October 1973, p. 9.

30. Orwell, "The Principles of Newspeak," p. 310.

31. The article, "One Small Step for Genkind," published in the *New York Times Magazine,* April 16, 1972, is reprinted in this volume following the Postscript.

32. Varda One, "Manglish," *Everywoman,* October 23, 1970.

33. Culpepper proposed *gynergy* in "Female History/Myth Making," *The Second Wave,* Spring 1975, Vol. 4, No. 1; Sheldon proposed *phallustine* in a Letter to the Editor, *The Village Voice,* December 17, 1970; and Strainchamps used WASM in "Our Sexist Language," p. 244.

34. The Shakespeare and Shaw quotations are from the Oxford English Dictionary, under the entries *themselves* and *their,* respectively; the Fitzgerald quotation is from Ethel Strainchamps's citation files.

35. As quoted in Nadine Brozan, "For Decades, a Voice of Reason on Sex," *New York Times,* June 28, 1974, p. 39.

36. The Lord Chesterfield quotation is from the Oxford English Dictionary, under the entry *they;* the Kennedy and Lessing quotations are from Ethel Strainchamps's citation files; and the Hart quotation was broadcast on the "CBS Evening News," February 6, 1975.

37. Otto Jespersen, *Growth and Structure of the English Language,* Garden City, N.Y., Doubleday & Company, Doubleday Anchor Books, 1955, p. 250. (First published in 1905.)

CHAPTER 9 LANGUAGE AND LIBERATION

1. Helen Keller, *The Story of My Life,* p. 36.

2. Edward Sapir, *Culture, Language, and Personality,* David G. Mandelbaum, ed., Berkeley and Los Angeles, University of California Press, 1966, pp. 68–69.

3. Benjamin Lee Whorf, *Language, Thought, and Reality: Selected Writings of Benjamin Lee Whorf,* John Carroll, ed., New York, M.I.T. Press and John Wiley & Sons, 1956, p. 240.

4. Encyclopædia Britannica, 1971 ed., p. 76C.

5. The material on the Avilik, including the passage by Edmund Car-

penter, is from Roy A. Gallant, *Man Must Speak: The Story of Language and How We Use It,* New York, Random House, 1969, pp. 150–52.

6. Warren Farrell, *The Liberated Man,* New York, Random House, 1974, pp. xxxi–xxxii.

7. Howard Husock, "Wanted: A Lover by Any Other Name," *The Boston Phoenix,* July 16, 1974, p. 13.

8. Fitzhugh Dodson, *How to Father,* Los Angeles, Nash Publishing, 1974.

9. Edward Sapir, *Language: An Introduction to the Study of Speech,* New York, Harcourt, Brace & World, Harvest Books, 1949, p. 17. (First published in 1921.)

10. Sandra L. and Daryl J. Bem, "Women's Role in American Society: Retrospect and Prospect," as reprinted in *Women's Role in Contemporary Society: The Report of the New York City Commission on Human Rights, September 21–25, 1970,* New York, Avon Books, Discus Edition, 1972, p. 102.

11. Sophie Drinker, *Music and Women: The Story of Women in Their Relation to Music,* New York, Coward-McCann, 1948, p. 266.

12. The material on the American Heritage School Dictionary is from Alma Graham, "The Making of a Nonsexist Dictionary," *Ms.,* December 1973.

13. "Guidelines for Improving the Image of Women in Textbooks," Scott, Foresman, pp. 5, 8.

14. Elizabeth Burr, Susan Dunn, and Norma Farquhar, "Equal Treatment of the Sexes in Social Studies Textbooks: Guidelines for Author and Editors," photocopy of typescript, 1972, p. 6.

15. "Imprint," magazine for McGraw-Hill authors published by McGraw-Hill, Spring 1975, p. 2.

16. Personal correspondence of Hubbard H. Cobb.

17. Elizabeth Dickinson, "The Word Game," *Canadian Library Journal,* August 1974, p. 339.

18. The position paper by Joan K. Marshall was reprinted in the Hennepin County Library's *Cataloging Bulletin* #11/12/13, March 15, 1975, pp. 10–11.

19. The American Library Association resolution was reported in *Media Report to Women,* May 1, 1975, p. 10.

20. U.S. Department of Labor, Office of Information, news release for November 9, 1973: "52 Job Titles Revised to Eliminate Sex-Stereotyping."

21. Mary M. Fuller, "In Business, the Generic Pronoun 'He' Is Non-Job Related and Discriminatory," *Training and Development Journal,* May 1973, p. 10.

22. Linda Charlton, "Rights Scoreboard," *New York Times,* November 18, 1973, the "Week in Review" section.

23. "Obey Thy Husband," *Time* magazine, May 20, 1974, p. 64.

24. Minutes of the Ninth General Synod, United Church of Christ, St. Louis, Mo., June 22–26, 1973.

25. *Gates of Prayer: The New Union Prayerbook,* New York, Central Conference of American Rabbis, 1975, pp. xii, 229, 254–55, 257, and 265.

26. In addition to the several religious bodies and communities in the process of revising their printed materials, the Division of Education and Ministries of the National Council of Churches sponsored "The Liberating Word: A Guide to Non-Sexist Interpretation of the Bible," Letty M. Russell, ed., Philadelphia, Westminster Press, 1976.

27. "Linguistic Sexism," editorial, *Journal of Ecumenical Studies,* Vol. XI, No. 2, Spring 1974.

28. Ibid.

29. Oxford English Dictionary, under the entry *harlot.*

30. William Shakespeare, *The Winter's Tale,* Act III, Scene 3.

31. Oxford English Dictionary, under the entry *fellow.*

32. Quoted from Michael Korda, *Male Chauvinism!* New York, Random House, 1973, by Jo Ann Levine, "Male Chauvinism—As a Male Analyzes It," *Christian Science Monitor,* July 29, 1973.

33. Margaret Mead, *Male and Female: A Study of the Sexes in a Changing World,* New York, Dell Publishing Company, Laurel Edition, 1968, p. 351. (First published in 1949.)

34. Webster's Third New International Dictionary of the English Language, 1986, under the entry *castration complex.*

35. Orwell, "Politics and the English Language," pp. 109, 110–11.

36. Harvey Cox, "Of Witches and Pagans, Female," *New York Times,* October 1, 1973, p. 35.

37. Orwell, "Politics and the English Language," pp. 109, 114.

INDEX

Words referred to as words, both English and foreign, are set in italic type. The letter "n" indicates a numbered note on the page indicated.